BOLD REINVENTED

NEXT LEVEL LEADING WITH COURAGE, CONSCIOUSNESS AND CONVICTION

ZANA GOIC PETRICEVIC

FOREWORD BY LIBERTO PEREDA, VP EUROPE OF THE LEADERSHIP CIRCLE®

Cover image by: Ryanurz, 99 Designs
Book design by: SWATT Books Ltd

ISBN: 978-953-49612-0-9 (Paperback)
ISBN: 978-953-49612-1-6 (eBook)

Publisher: Bold Leadership Culture d.o.o.
Alagoviceva 14, 10 000 Zagreb, Croatia

Zagreb, 2021

www.boldleadership-culture.com

For all game changers.

And for Noa, who I know will always dare to swim upstream.

Advance praise

When I read the advance copy of *Bold Reinvented*, I was nudged to ask myself "What is mine to do to make this world a better place?"
Through brilliant concepts and compelling story telling, Zana has taken the leadership conversation to a much-needed next level.
I recommend this book to all global citizens who are called to be a different kind of leader. As Zana points out, our world is craving for game changers. This book will inspire you to find your worthy cause, discover your meaningful work, and leave a legacy. If you long to impact our world, and discover your own bold leadership, this is a must read. You matter, and your work matters!
Rick Tamlyn
Master Certified Coach (MCC), author of Play Your Bigger Game

Very inspiring book showing how through personal challenges one can develop courage to be truly self. Reading it you find your own questions and the answers appear right in front of you. This book just step by step shows how to fire up your innate guidance system and have courage to follow your bold direction in life and find wonder in every day being on your journey.
Joanna Antkiewicz
PwC CEE Head of Coaching and Wellbeing, ICF Master Certified Coach

A bold leader is in many ways naked. Reading this book, we will come to the conclusion that for bold leaders there is no dressing up or hiding behind great creations of status. Fancy clothing will rip on the climb up the leadership hill. You are what you are, and you do what you do. You do not hide behind anything. Everything is visible in your visions and actions. After reading and embracing this book you will dare to lead with what you were born with.

Bold Reinvented takes you on a journey to your own wisdom so you can discover, understand and be amazed by the bold leader within yourself. The gap most of us encounter between our power and our wisdom can be very concerning, but now Zana brings to us the most promising possibilities. She doesn't tell us what to do, but opens new bold ways to think – so that we instinctively know what to do. And this new knowledge will stay in our system long after other management buzzes have faded.

Mirjam Johansson Grant

Leadership coach, organisational consultant and CEO of DevelUpment AB

When you make the decision to write a book – a really good book – then it's one hell of a ride. Not only do you need to uncover the value of what you know, you have to extract it out of your head in a way that best serves you and your reader. It can get complicated. Messy. And frustrating at times.

It can dredge up difficult experiences, which need to be dealt with, but equally, there's a magic that happens when you truly realise and accept your gold, your achievements, and bring them alive.

It's been a pleasure to support Zana as she has written her book. Not only has she written it in a language that's not her mother tongue, but she has also eloquently crafted her words in a way that will make you think, connect the dots and transform the way you lead.

She clearly demonstrates how her own experiences have impacted her life, but without these, she would not be here today encouraging you to step up and be bold. And through writing her book, I've seen her blossom and step into her own bold leadership, which means she can show you how it's done!

Karen Williams

The Book Mentor, bestselling author of six books and TEDx speaker

Zana Goic Petricevic has written an important book about leadership and about being a human being: How can we find the courage to live full lives and stop playing small?
What I love about the book is that it integrates important perspectives on leadership into a holistic conversation about the messy process we all engage in when we debate with ourselves whether to take the risk and follow our passion or stay safe, comfortable and protected. Making fundamental changes brings discomfort and sometimes pain; the bigger the leap the greater the pain. Zana beautifully describes the processes of "self disruption" where, in order to move to another level, we have to give up things we believe to be true in order to move into a space where nothing is certain – and it is precisely this uncertainty that is the path to greatness. The author is encouraging us all to be bold and take the leap, because it is in discovering our passion/purpose and daring to play it big that we will have the real impact that the world needs.
The book is deep and soulful and triggers important reflections and conversations. It is also a practical book where the author holds the reader's hand and coaches them in discovering the path to their own boldness. Finally, it is a personal book where Zana's own story, and those of several of her clients, give life and context to the SOUL framework, a great stepwise framework for developing your own leadership in radical connection with others.
Ingunn Vagstein
Partner at ViiB, Global Faculty Partner and Trainer at Barrett Values Centre and certified systems coach (ORSC)

A fascinating book. With a confident style Zana weaves together clear theory and inspiring stories to explain what a bolder leader is and how you can become one. This book will prompt you to consider powerful questions and it is a beautiful invitation to self-reflection.
Raluca Andreea Popa, PhD
Professor at Bucharest University of Economic Studies

This book speaks truth: I now dare to know what bold leaders look and feel like. Thank you for putting your wisdom and passion into words. You combine deep wisdom, brilliant observations, personal stories and practical tips to get our SOULs started: what an achievement! The quote from Doug Conant has never been truer: Your life story is your leadership story.

Inger Beate Botheim

Partner and co-founder of ViiB

This is a must-read book for all leaders who would like to make a transformative change in their world and are aware that the only way to achieve this is by a continuous and highly dedicated self-reflective practice on one side, and a strong constant commitment to being the greatest version of themselves on the other.

This publication is more than just another book. Through the author's personal reflections, the leaders' stories, and their challenges, and well-elaborated leadership concepts, the publication guides you through your own leadership transformation journey. If you thoroughly consider the reflective questions provided by the author, by the time you finish reading this book, you will understand clearly what your story and your purpose are, and what the change needed to be made in your world by you is.

I highly recommend this book to all leaders who seek meaning in the world and who are brave enough to start passionately creating bolder working environments and more daring societies.

Dr. Alenka Braček Lalić

Founder and Managing Director of AUTHENTIC LEADERSHIP Institute, co-editor of Hidden Champions in Dynamically Changing Societies: Critical Success Factors for Market Leadership *and* Business and Society: Making Management Education Relevant for the 21st Century

I have read many articles, blog posts and books where the author is "reinventing ____" (fill in the blank). When I first read the title of Zana's work "Bold Reinvented", my initial thought was, who better to write a book about "bold" than Zana! What a terrific read and the title aptly reflects my experience working with Zana. She is a leader who embodies, both literally and figuratively, the essence of bold leadership. The list from the chapter "Jumpstart your bold leadership" is an exceptional tool for sustaining the many valuable lessons from this book.

John W. Sigmon

CEO and activist, Sigmon Leadership Solutions

The title of *Bold Reinvented* already sets the stage for a book that has a lot to live up to and Zana doesn't disappoint. With her wise, evocative words, astute observations and sharing of her own courageously vulnerable stories ("none of us can separate our leadership from our personal experiences"), Zana takes us on a discovery ... and calling forth ... of our own Bold Leadership in service of our SELF (our "raw human magnificence"), our "radical humanity" and connection with OTHERS, our unshakeable contribution and service to our wider UNIVERSE and LEGACY. Throughout the pages, Zana makes powerful and compelling cases for taking these Bold steps, peppering them with examples of those who have previously paved such untrodden paths. She leaves us with no option but to leap and so read at your own peril of making positive, courageous change!!

Biba Binotti

CEO Global Warriors

Contents

ADVANCE PRAISE **5**

FOREWORD **15**

PROLOGUE **17**
- School of hard knocks 17
  - Personal curriculum 21
  - Making sense 25

INTRODUCTION **29**
- Practical and reflective 30
- SOUL framework 31
- Other concepts and theories 33
- Stories 35
- Vision, discomfort and the soul work 35
- Who this book is for 37

PART 1 – SELF **39**
- Liberating boldness 40

CHAPTER 1: HUNGER FOR LEARNING **43**
- Personal leadership development 44
- The daring upgrade 47
- The how 53

The why 56

Your reflection 63

CHAPTER 2: THE ART OF SELF-DISRUPTION **65**

Cracking the code 67

Illusionary safety 70

The choice of disarming illusions 72

Your reflection 75

CHAPTER 3: BECOMING **77**

Accepting your old story 79

Own a new story 83

Next level Self 85

Your reflection 86

PART 2 – OTHER **89**

Where leadership lives 90

CHAPTER 4: SEEING ME **95**

Reflection of me 96

Impatient for your flaws 98

Oneness 102

Your reflection 105

CHAPTER 5: TRUSTING **107**

Integrity 108

Intimacy 110

Allowing 114

Empowering nature of trust 119

Your reflection 123

CHAPTER 6: CALLING FORTH **125**

Hard-loving truth 126

My longing for you 128

Leaning into each other 132

Your reflection 134

PART 3 – UNIVERSE	**135**
A home we don't want to live in	136
CHAPTER 7: THE CONCERN	**141**
Two promises	141
The charm of conformity	144
Unreasonableness	146
Your reflection	149
CHAPTER 8: THE VOICE	**151**
Unspoken	152
Seated in the midst of fire	156
Bolder conversation	160
Your reflection	164
CHAPTER 9: THE CONTRIBUTION	**165**
Non-authority leadership	166
The practice of questioning	166
Power and wisdom gap	168
Your reflection	174
PART 4 – LEGACY	**175**
The work you love	176
CHAPTER 10: MEANINGFUL WORK	**181**
The conversation about meaning	182
Purposeful achievement	187
Our soul's love	193
Your reflection	194
CHAPTER 11: THE COMMITMENT	**195**
The expression	196
The vision and the discomfort	202
Your reflection	203

CHAPTER 12: GAME CHANGERS 205
Next level boldness 206
Call to bold action now 210
Your reflection 213

EPILOGUE 215

JUMPSTART YOUR BOLD LEADERSHIP 221

APPENDIX 229

NOTES 235

RECOMMENDED READING 243

ACKNOWLEDGEMENTS 247

ABOUT THE AUTHOR 249

Foreword

IN MY ROLE as Vice President and Regional Faculty Lead at the Leadership Circle, I've met hundreds of coaches, all committed to the same mission: evolving the conscious practice of leadership. Our societies are in urgent need of conscious leaders, like you, bringing the full potency of their leadership, bringing their soul.

I met Zana for the first time in November 2019 when she was participating in the Collective Leadership Assessment Certification, her second accreditation with the Leadership Circle. In one of the breaks, she approached me, and shared her mission with me: "I want to contribute to conscious leadership in my region, for a better world." Her bold statement and her determination impacted me in a deep way. After that day, many conversations and exchanges followed. Every single time, she was holding the same noble sense of urgency for the fulfillment of her mission.

Zana, like you, wants to make a difference and is fully committed to take leadership whenever it might be needed. She always leads with the intention of having a positive impact for a better world for all of us and especially for the next generations.

Over the last decades, it has been commonly accepted that this kind of leadership was to be provided by senior leaders in charge of global affairs, whether in the public or the private sectors. However, the times for waiting for direction from the top are gone, and millions of people around the planet are being evoked to stand up and take the lead at the very local level. Even people who held themselves as followers are urged to enact the role of leadership.

Zana's book should not be necessary, because boldness and leadership are somehow synonyms. However, this is seldom the case. When looking at most companies and governments, one can easily realize that there's a mismatch between the announced purpose and the actual practice of leadership in the world. Walking the talk is not that common. Leaders must pay serious and honest attention to this mismatch, to not let bold leadership be a paradox. The stakes are high.

This takes bold leadership. At all levels, global, continental, national and local, we are called to have real and meaningful impact and we cannot afford "greenwashed" leadership anymore.

Hence, Zana's book is very needed and comes at the right time. Whether you are about to step into leadership, or you are a consolidated leader, by reading this book, and very especially by doing the work Zana invites us all to do, you will feel evoked to contemplate your own leadership mismatch. You will be stepping into self-authoring your leadership journey.

Zana will guide you through the book, one step at a time, with gentleness and boldness, with love and compassion, yet challenge you in many ways. This is how she shows up in her leadership and in her coaching practice, genuine, bold and true to her soul.

As you read the book, keep in your heart that place or problem you really care about, and then work boldly on it, putting into action all that you will discover about yourself, about your bold leadership.

Liberto Pereda
VP Europe of The Leadership Circle®

Prologue

School of hard knocks

IT WAS 2011, just a few days before Christmas. I came to work that morning and sat at my desk looking at nearly a hundred emails received just the day before when suddenly the screen went black. I took a deep sigh, thinking how this was the very last thing I needed.

Still gazing at the black screen, I extended my right arm to pick up the phone and reach out to my PA for support. My hand stopped somewhere in the air above the handset as the phone surprised me by ringing in that very moment. I picked it up in confusion, without looking at the display, and heard her voice. I immediately went: "Oh good, it's you – I really need you to try and reach one of the IT people as quickly as you can..."

She interrupted me. In a deadly serious tone of voice, that I'd never heard from her in all the four years of us working together, she said, "The Head of Security is in front of your door and he insists on seeing you."

"Well, if he insists, then let him in," I said in surprise and went back to what I thought was really more important for me in that moment. "Do try to find someone to check what is happening with my computer please."

And the Head of Security came in. He was a nice old chap, always ready to joke and bring what you could call a positive energy. At least that had been my experience. He had been managing the security department for about two years at the time, since he had joined the company. Given his age I guess this was supposed to be his last position before he ended his career to take a well-deserved retirement.

Our offices were on the 5th floor, along the corridor from the Chairman to whom we both reported. We would bump into each other a number of times during the day as we walked in and out of our offices and each time, he would tell a joke that lit up the day.

This time he entered my office with no smile on his face. I stood up from my desk and walked towards him as he came in. Before I even managed to offer my hand for a handshake, he spoke in a linear, emotionless voice: "Collect your personal belongings and leave this building at once. The Chairman has lost his trust in you."

I paused. In shock. I bet I even stopped breathing.

The Chairman he was referring to was already the third one I had reported to in my four years as Head of Corporate Communications, which was half the time I'd spent at the company. We had collaborated well for over a year, before it became obvious that our very fundamental sets of values were so different and almost impossible to align. I had dared to confront him, and this situation made it clear that my approach on the most recent occasion had not been appreciated.

I stood looking into the familiar face of this man in an utterly unfamiliar role. At the sound of his request, my feet felt they were losing the ground beneath them. If I had to use one word to describe this experience, I'd say that it was one of helplessness.

I stood there speechless, my sense of security utterly shattered, my sense of self diminished. I felt numb. I do not recall how long those moments lasted, but I am aware that the intensity of my experience in that instant could have made them feel much longer than they actually were.

In any case, somewhere amid my own mental repetition of what he had told me to do, I heard his voice again: "Collect your personal belongings and leave this building at once." This time I managed to respond. I remember taking a step to my right in order to place my hand on my desk as if looking for something to rely on, as I spoke: "I'm not sure what exactly you are violating in this moment, but I'm sure you are violating some of my human rights." I just spoke from exactly how it felt for me: a threat against me as a person.

He looked at me and said: "If this is not going to go smoothly, I can also call the police to get it over with." That gave me another kick of reality, this time with no trace of politeness, and it began to sound really absurd. I confronted him by inviting him to do so if he believed he had a valid reason for that.

It felt as if the over-inflated balloon popped in that moment and he went back to his point: "I've got to execute this and I've got to do it quickly." This time he said it as if he was expecting to receive empathy from me. Of course, I wasn't able to empathise with him at that moment. Today I am able to understand him as a human being that operated from a reactive place of his own self-protection. The reaction that has us humans choose comfort over courage.[1] And so, I guess, even good people sometimes do things that do not look exactly right.

I was aware enough to request the possibility of making one phone call and he allowed me to do so. I consulted with a friend of mine who I knew had immediate access to a lawyer and I got off the call knowing I must not leave my office without being handed an official company decision that put this request in writing.

My inflexibility around this request created quite a fuss. It made the situation more complex and it also made it last for as long as five hours, during which time I was not allowed to leave the office unless I was going to leave the building without that piece of paper. It was altogether a very unpleasant experience.

Then someone came in to hand me the written decision, according to which I had to leave the building, and was restricted from accessing any company premises until further notice. To bottom-line this experience: this entire situation and the way it developed beyond that point made me grow to experience previously unimagined dimensionalities of my own boldness.

My company laptop and mobile phone were taken away from me, but I was allowed to drive away in my company car, which I did leaving behind almost a decade of what I knew to be hard work and commitment. The gate closed behind me and it was really the end of one story and pretty much one identity of mine that I'd known until then.

The reason I say the end of my identity is because, being driven by hard work and results for my entire life by then, I'd established my sense of worth and security through task accomplishment, personal achievement and control of what I did.

My job was my life, my world. For me, there was no other more important focus in my reality. And then suddenly, my reality was completely contrary to what I understood was making me worthy and safe: it was a punishment, not an accomplishment, and I was in no control over what was happening. It was a failure. And I was a failure because of it. Leadership Circle Profile™[2] and the Immunity to Change Map would later on help me uncover this and many other deeply-seated limiting assumptions through which I was making sense of the world.

I also found much comfort in reading the work of Viktor Frankl, the father of logotherapy, who said that the last of the human freedoms was to choose one's attitude in any given set of circumstances. Therefore, when we are no longer in the position to change the situation, we can always change ourselves.

That is, obviously, easier said than done. Because what was happening for me was pretty much this: my identity died that day but I resisted burying it for as long as a few years afterwards. And as I resisted burying my identity that was no longer alive, I refused to change myself. As I refused to change myself, I rejected learning. As I rejected learning, I was not integrating many important parts of myself. As I failed to integrate them, I was not being whole.

And as I was not being whole, I felt broken. And that meant I felt as if I had done something terribly wrong, that kept me feeling guilty and ashamed.

My life went on; I got married, two years later we had our son, I had two stepchildren, I had wonderful parents, I even had a job, and all along I also had something that felt not completely alive, something like a hole in my soul.

Personal curriculum

In *An Everyone Culture*, a book co-authored by two Harvard faculty members, Robert Kegan and Lisa Laskow Lahey, there is a powerful quote by Bryan Ungard, a Chief Purpose Officer of Decurion, a company presented in the book as the deliberately developmental organisation. Ungard says: "Feast on your imperfections, or starve on your ego."[3]

In 2016, I started feasting on my imperfections and going through the lessons of my "personal curriculum", to use the term from the book.

I opened up to deep, vulnerable and continuous learning. I'm not exaggerating when I say that it brought me a whole new life because it created a whole new me; it changed me. What I mean by this is that it changed the choices I make in life, and that was mostly because it changed my decision-making pattern and generally the way I make sense of my world.

I realised that I was somehow always choosing what made me feel safe over what made me feel really alive. I had to admit that I was in the habit of choosing conformity over integrity. And that was obviously easy to accept as a strategy that successfully supported my corporate life ambition, but now that that reality had ended, there was not much aliveness I was left with. This was also because my sense of aliveness in my corporate career was rarely a passion; it was rather a drive. In my new reality, I began to differentiate between those two.

I decided to treat myself to a coaching class weekend in London to help me get some clarity around what was next for me and I selected the city that has always been inspiring for me. It was a trip that required me to go to my savings account for financial resources, which was again beyond my comfortable level of safety. I faced my demons and eventually jumped on the plane!

You may call it a coincidence. I call it support from the universe that comes as a reward for your own daring. I googled this: coaching training London UK. Google offered: CTI UK[4]. CTI brought me an adventure of a lifetime and opened up whole new horizons! Apart from CTI, there was only one other coaching school that caught my attention. That school was not offering classes that year. Draw your own conclusions around coincidences.

After the first weekend, I signed up for six months of training with CTI in London. After the six months, I signed up for an additional half year of CTI coaching certification. As I was developing my own coaching consciousness, what grew in me was a tremendous desire to bring this mindset to the corporate space, this way of seeing self and other people, this way of empowering self and others, this way of opening and having conversations. I wished I had previously had this mindset to be able to see people through those eyes and be seen that way myself.

Coaching can seem very fluffy for the corporate arena once you start learning it, but there's absolutely nothing fluffy about coaching when you get the right language. And the right language was the Universal Model of Leadership™ as a leadership philosophy that comes to life through two assessment tools: Leadership Circle Profile™ and Collective Leadership Assessment™.[5] Boy, did that training restructure every cell of my being! Later on, combined with the Immunity to Change Map, a method developed by Robert Kegan and Lisa Laskow Lahey, it showed me the windows I look through to make sense of the world: deep-seated limiting and hurting assumptions driven by my fears and my human need for safety. It was scary and liberating at the same time.

It's beautiful when an individual starts an inner path to change. Still, we don't live in isolation, and neither do we live in the training rooms where magic happens. Once we leave the bubble of the development course we get hit by the reality of our workplaces, our families, our world. And my family reality was challenging at the time. I was living in a blended marriage in which everyone had their own pain. Systems dynamics is not something we can change through power and control, but we can understand the way it works to facilitate change. So, I started a total of fourteen months of Organisation and Relationship Systems Coaching[6] that forever changed the way I look at any relationship. Forever. It's a paradigm shift in looking at any workplace team or any other relationship. It's not an easy mindset to welcome, but it is a healing path to collaborative co-existence in any context.

And finally, at the end of 2018, somewhere in the middle of my initial learning and final certifying to understand and work with systems, I made a decision that once again changed my life and affected all of my choices because it pulled me once again to the next level. I started the ten-month-long experiential leadership development programme with the Co-Active Training Institute. I had two MBA degrees – a Croatian one and a UK one – when I joined this course. Two degrees that taught me nothing about leading myself or others in the sense of how to create the empowering culture as a leader to unlock both human and business potential. This leadership training dismantled me into pieces, me and my views on leadership, and then it delivered the next level of me in summer 2019.

These are just the key training pillars that re-created me, alongside which there were a number of books, concepts, theories and learning groups of people that became a regular part of my life. Alongside these, there were a number of individual clients, teams and groups that I was working with and bringing this new knowledge to. I travelled more in those four years than I had in my entire life. My network of like-minded colleagues and friends grew with people from all continents and all backgrounds. I've experienced what it means to deeply connect to yourself and others, to really make this world better together. What it means to be fearless and free. What it means to be alive. I've experienced passion, not drive. And as I felt passionate about who I was becoming, I experienced safety as an inner feeling. It was my inner authority that I started to rely on to access safety.

It's important to understand that this does not mean my life stopped being complex. On the contrary, I believe it got even more so. I was handling family, getting trained in something I'd never done up to that point, setting up a new business, and navigating tons of different expectations my world had of me.

I was also facing the issue of the different images people around me had of me and I realised that I wasn't the only one who once found it difficult to let go of my past identity. It was very difficult for many of my closest friends and family too; for some of them I know it still is. Some of them have a hard time handling my "new" risk-taking character. Some of them still refuse to accept that I'd exchange any sense of status-based power to feel, if only a bit, empowerment and aliveness myself and the blessing of helping others to experience it.

My reality was, and still is, overly complex and overpacked, to say the least. But my learning journey has given me a different level of consciousness to meet many of my complex realities in a different way. In a bolder way.

I've come to understand again through experience that aliveness, freedom, boldness and safety are inner feelings. That's why it's not easy to define the true experience of them. One simply has to experience them! But what can be clearly defined is that there is no way you can purchase them or deceive yourself into having those feelings. You experience them by walking towards what really matters to you in any context – in your corporate career or elsewhere. It's not about the setting. It's about the readiness to take risks for what's important to you as against conforming to not lose what somebody else says is important for you. It's a road that takes you from conformity to true integrity and that road is paved with risk. The risk of speaking up and doing something, anything, when all other voices inside and outside you say: Don't. You mustn't. It's not safe. Control yourself. Control your passions. Control your life.

In his book *The Answer to How is Yes*, Peter Block says: "Choosing to act on what matters is the choice to live a passionate existence, which is anything but controlled and predictable."[7]

I believe that given the uncontrollable and unpredictable nature of life, it's never about knowing what the right answer is. It's about asking what the thing is that matters to us so much that we're willing to take the risk and keep going through discomfort to follow our vision, by choice.

The programmes that formed part of my personal and professional coaching and leadership development changed my life, because they changed me. They helped me choose a life in which what I honour is the hunger for a state of constant enquiry: not the right answers, but the right questions that have the power to support me in my leadership work in the most fulfilling way.

I lost my management job and ended my corporate career in quite a state of discomfort, only to realise that I had such important leadership work to do that in fact I reinvented my identity. As quickly as I turned that work into my current coaching and leadership development, speaking and writing business, I did it this time with the crystal clear knowledge that there is a huge difference between how one decides to approach the job that one does and the work that one has in the world.

Life obviously continues to seriously challenge in me what is at the core of any decision-making process for every human being: the tension between what makes me feel safe and what makes me feel alive.

What I know today, while always being open to learn more, is how to access my inner capacity to resolve this tension so as to create the next level of me that absolutely every single time feels almost inconceivably bolder. And more ***alive***.

Making sense

There is a scene in the 2017 epic fantasy adventure film *King Arthur: Legend of the Sword*, when Arthur finally defeats the villain, his uncle Vortigern, and just before he kills him says to him: "You make sense of the devil."

That is a wonderful metaphor for what we are all really searching for in life – the meaning of everything that happens: all the devils and all the gods.

Einstein said that there is only one road to human greatness, and that is through the school of hard knocks. I believe that human greatness is the ultimate unlocking of our potential to do our work in service of the world – not our job, our work – and that as part of that process we also really need to make sense of our hard knock lessons.

We need to find the meaning of what happens in our life and work. And we will, if we look for it.

What has helped me is to know that life is a choice in the sense that I can choose my response to it. If life is a choice, it also means that life is an opportunity. And when we're offered an opportunity, it requires us to be responsible as to what we do with it; this is responsibility not in the sense of being a burden, but being the context that one chooses to live in: "...a grace you give yourself, an empowering context that leaves you with a say in the matter of life"[8].

Our circumstances may often be hard knock, devilish lessons, but we do still have a say.

Now, to engage with this opportunity that I was offered, it was essential for me to understand living as a process of endless becoming of the next level of self, that self that would do the next level of my work in service of the next level of my world.

This process of endless next level becoming, which is in fact the process of growing and the point of which is to equip us for our next possible, next reality, next work in our world, is deeply anchored in our integrity. Now, here's how I've come to understand integrity in the process of writing this book. Integrity stands for all that I am in my very core, and therefore also all that I can be, and all that I can create from that space.

If that's what integrity holds, then I believe our integrity is seated in our souls. And much of our life's dilemma is whether we are bold enough to follow our soul desires, to follow what we know in our souls that we are, what we can be, and what we can create. Because what our soul desires do – more often than not – is represent a risk. Or an opportunity, depending on how you choose to look at it.

There's a powerful message I once read that says "I'd rather walk around naked than wear a coat the world has made for me"[9]. What I've realised from my story is, you don't have to walk around naked. We equally don't have to walk around conforming and wearing other people's creations. We have a choice, which means an opportunity and a responsibility to keep creating our own coats to wear that truly serve us, so that we can do our work serving our world in what we all find meaningful. Acting on that choice is called leadership.

With my coaching consciousness, there is little nowadays that I claim is the unconditional truth, but I do here: that choice is not always the most comfortable, but at the level of your soul it does always make sense.

So, am I on the right path now? I dare to know I am[10], but who knows if I'm right. What I do know is that I'm on such a passionate path now and that what once felt like a hole in my soul, now feels like – at moments almost palpably – my soul fullness!

Introduction

BOLDNESS TAKES YOUR soul fullness.

Let me tell you what that means and what I believe. Bold leadership requires you to engage your entire soul in what you bring as a leader. Your soul is the home of everything that is meaningful for you and as such it is the source of knowing all you need to know to boldly do your leadership work, that with which you serve the larger context of the world.

It is from your soul that you know the ***why*** to every decision you make as a leader. And it is from that very place that you feel it is the right decision, even when you don't really know if you are right about it. You simply dare to know it, and that daring by itself is completely impossible to comprehend from any other source of intelligence in you other than your soul.

Because here's the truth: you cannot be bold from your head. There is a limit to the boldness that comes from your rational mind.

Your mind will frequently stop you and tell you to be cautious. It will warn you that it is too dangerous or even impossible to do your leadership work. It won't even give you complete clarity around what your leadership work really is that you need to bring to your world, the reason for which you exist here in the first place. Because it will be too busy handling the risk.

Your soul, on the other hand, will invite you to do what feels deeply meaningful despite all the risk. That makes your soul the only place where you can access your limitless bold leadership.

This book will show you the steps of how to bring this belief to life in your leadership.

It will introduce you to the potential that I have given to the concept of bold leadership and show you how boldness comes to its full expression, its full life, through the courage, consciousness and convictions that leaders bring to the table as they're serving their world. As it shows you different dimensions of bold leadership, this book will also teach you how to access them.

My longing for your leadership in our world is that this book leaves you believing this statement: to be a bold leader takes the entire SOUL.

Practical and reflective

This book will approach the question of how to bring your entire soul to your leadership in two ways.

One of them is a practical approach that offers you a framework to follow in your leadership.

The other is a reflective approach based on my conviction that the risk of bold leadership, the reinvented one our world desperately needs, requires all of us to do our deep soul work.

In purely practical terms this means that it requires leaders to be in a state of constant enquiry about their life and leadership and rely on their soul to discover the most meaningful answers to who they are, where they are going and why, and thus make sense of the risk of their actions.

The two approaches - practical and reflective - relate to each other: applying the SOUL framework in your leadership will support you in constantly doing your soul work and your soul work will help you bring your meaningful leadership to life through the framework.

In offering these two approaches that work in collaboration, this book aims to shift both the acting and thinking, doing and being of its readers, their individual leadership that creates our collective one.

SOUL framework

Let's first start with the practical approach. As mysterious as it may sound, bringing your entire soul to your leadership happens through a very clear path. Not an easy one, but clear to the point that your logical brain can call it a framework. It's a framework that may have its usual sequence of steps, but in fact you can start walking from any point as long as you do, and as you start walking you will visit all of its parts throughout the journey.

This framework is called SOUL and its parts are ***Self***, ***Other***, ***Universe*** and ***Legacy***. As you move further into this book, I will sometimes refer to them as realms of leadership. Now, let's go back to how you actually bring the fullness of your soul to your leadership through this framework.

It usually starts with the realm of ***Self*** because none of us can separate our own leadership from our own self, our own identity. In fact, it starts with confronting our own self first, which means raising awareness of our needs and desires, and then our comfort zones, our limiting assumptions, and finally our old and new stories.

Part 1 of this book will show you what is confronting about this work, and how that serves you. It will put you into the most uncomfortable shoes of a leader who is a learner rather than an expert or a knower.

It will also make you realise that you as a leader need to be on the constant lookout for what the next level of your work in the world is, even in the middle of your busy personal and professional circumstances.

Self is where you deal with all the questions of creating and re-creating your next level, a self that is big and bold enough to support you in doing your leadership work.

The next step, Part 2 of the SOUL, is ***Other***. This is the part that teaches you what is contrary to how your brain works.

Neuroscience research will tell you that our brains are capable of making a decision about how trustworthy other people are in a split second, which means that our brains immediately judge. ***Other*** as a realm of leadership will teach you a new definition of leadership that says: leadership is a radical connection.

What that actually means and why it is called radical is because it does not first invite us to discover whether we can trust other people or not, but it invites us to consciously make ourselves wired to immediately look for the wisdom in other people, which will automatically make us both wiser. And then also to hold this approach constantly, even in the middle of confrontation.

Other will take your leadership from transactional to relational.

By the time you've read these two parts, I dare to know that you'll experience a few significant paradigm shifts that will empower you, which is a wonderful moment to start reading Part 3, that is called ***Universe*** and describes leadership as a matter of concern, not a matter of formal power.

Universe will bring your focus to the systems in which you operate, your family, your organisation, your team, your community, and it will take your accountability for them to the next level. It will teach you how to use your voice to initiate change. It will help you differentiate between two often colliding concepts: authority and leadership.

And finally, Part 4, ***Legacy***. ***Legacy*** in the SOUL framework comes at the end, but in reality, it begins with the very first step you've taken.

This part will help you understand many Ls in your life: are you making a Living, are you creating a Legacy, are you Loving what you do?

Legacy will point you to evolving your leadership from being operational to being truly visionary.

Other concepts and theories

In these four parts of the book that will walk you through the SOUL framework, you will get to know some concepts and tools that have, to a very large extent, impacted my own personal leadership development and my overall understanding of leadership.

One of the key leadership philosophies that I mention is the Universal Model of Leadership™, the backbone of which is Robert Kegan's Adult Development Theory, and its related assessment tool: Leadership Circle Profile™, used to assess individual leaders.[11]

This tool integrates some of the best leadership, psychological, and also spiritual development frameworks and theories into an assessment based on competencies that are correlated to leadership effectiveness and a business performance index.

In addition to its confirmed validity[12], the actual magic of this tool at presenting the deep, vulnerable and comprehensive human complexity of any leader that takes it is simply extraordinary.

I have never debriefed the results of this assessment with any leader who managed to stay untouched when seeing the gap between their own outer image and their own inner intentions as a leader that this tool so deeply and often painfully reveals.

It has therefore hugely shaped my coaching and leadership development practice and provided me with the right leadership language to bring to the world I used to be part of and which remains my focus in the work that I do – the corporate arena.

Leadership Circle Profile™ (LCP – for individual leaders), and the Collective Leadership Assessment™[13] (CLA – for leadership culture), as two transformative leadership development approaches, remain central to my work. In the Appendix of this book, you will learn more about their benefits for individual leaders and organisations as well as how to access your free Leadership Circle Profile™ self-assessment and contact me to discuss the results.

What you'll also hear me mention a few times throughout my book are some other authors and their words or views on leadership development.

The reason I do this is because they have contributed to the synergy of my experience in the leadership development field. They also continue to inspire me and pull my thinking to the next level of boldness from where I continue to create.

I believe these are fabulous works and, if you haven't already, I encourage you to explore them as additional sources of our higher collective leadership consciousness. You'll find them listed at the end of this book in the "Recommended reading" section.

Stories

This book will also take you through many stories to underpin the concepts that it offers. The one that you read in the Prologue will have given you an idea of how my own leadership transformation process started.

There are also elements of many other stories throughout the rest of the book that demonstrate the process of maturing our bold leadership through lots of enquiries and many risky steps. I may have modified certain elements of these stories in the service of absolutely protecting the confidentiality of my clients.

All these stories intend to show that leadership essentially is a risk. It is a process of holding a vision of what we wish to create, what we desire to make happen, and the discomfort of the risk it takes to do it.

Vision, discomfort and the soul work

Holding the vision and the discomfort at the same time is something that your logical brain can hardly make sense of because it does not feel comfortable with it, and it madly wants to restore the sense of comfort.

Because what it easily makes sense of are the steps that we take in the service of protection of ourselves and our basic needs for safety, certainty, belonging, status, authority, fairness; our needs to sort out the discomfort even at the expense of our vision. That's why it's not enough to engage only our head in this matter.

This book will ideally bring you closer to the belief that much of bold leadership is about daring to know what to do and which direction to go, when we cannot possibly be certain what the right answer really is. It's about clearly pursuing the path towards your vision and taking the discomfort of the uncertainty, again simply by daring to know that you are on the right path.

And here comes another important statement: there is something way bolder in us than our sense of logical knowing and our sense of power coming from our head.

For our heads, there is a missing piece in this puzzle called "dare to know". We have to look for it elsewhere in us. Our bigger self that is needed for our bolder work in the world requires us to find it and it is called – leadership.

At the end of the book, you will find the Epilogue, which attempts to leave you with the belief that everything that life offers to us is an invitation for our bigger self and our bolder leadership. It points you to two identities we ultimately choose to adopt as we live and lead: fighter or warrior. They come from different places, and they serve their worlds differently as a result of resolving the dilemma between what makes them feel safe and what makes them feel alive.

Our leadership work that makes us feel alive and serves the larger context of our world is risky. The soul work in our development helps us find meaning to this risk. Meaning to ***why*** and meaning to ***what now*** and then to ***what next***. Meaning to ***why us*** and then also to ***what for***.

It takes our entire human soul to make sense of the risk that's inherent in every true leadership. If you have studied some ancient religions, you can certainly speak much more than me about the qualities and meaning attributed to the human soul.

What I hope this book brings you is knowing that the only perfect element of anyone's leadership is their perfectly bold soul.

Who this book is for

So, who is this content for? Throughout the book, you will often hear me refer to corporate leaders simply because the corporate arena that I once belonged to remains the focus of my leadership development work. However, the SOUL framework and the accompanying ideas of this book target a much broader audience.

Therefore, this book is intended for current and future leaders, where leaders are defined as those that are in formal leadership positions in organisations and all the people that feel like leaders in their life and work without having any formal authority position.

The content in this book is the accumulation of my experience in the leadership development field, offered through my beliefs, ideas, concepts and stories. And while there is a flow to my thoughts and ideas, there is a lot to digest, so you may find you need to stop now and then to take in what you have read.

So, how could you read this book?

Rather than being a quick ***"how to"*** book, the majority of the content will invite you to take a deeper look into it, requiring you to pause, and perhaps come back to some parts until they are completely processed within you.

If I were to suggest one way of reading this book, it would be to proceed one chapter at the time, allowing not only for the book content to unfold but also to really land within you.

There are questions at the end of each chapter to help you with that. The intention is for these questions to serve as your companion, your SOUL-mate, your coach on this journey of becoming.

Allow yourself some time to pause and reflect on them, taking one chapter at a time as the book unfolds. Know that this is one of those books that you approach with depth rather than speed. As you do that, it will allow for your own courage, consciousness and conviction to boldly rise to the surface from deep within you.

In support of this rise, there are also key powerful beliefs throughout the entire book, some of which are listed for you at the very end of the book in the section "Jumpstart your bold leadership". The intention of this section is to provide you with the learning nuggets and inspiring quotes that you may wish to use to remind yourself and teach others how to bring bold leadership into their life and work.

And finally, my own dilemma.

I've learnt that an important approach in coaching and leadership development is to "meet others where they are". This is Co-Active coaching language that stands for approaching other people from what makes sense in their reality.

This is what I normally do in my leadership development work: I meet people where they are, get their attention and then I help them reach the next place in their development.

And yet in writing this book I had my own dilemma several times about whether I was approaching those who I imagine to be my readers from what makes sense in their reality, in terms of this book being useful to them.

I don't know the right answer, but I dare to know this: we won't reinvent bold leadership without a risk.

So, I'm taking the conscious risk of not comfortably meeting you where you are in the service of boldly inviting you to that next place where you can be. The next level of our world where we can in fact go together to continue reinventing bold leadership.

PART 1
SELF

Leadership begins by confronting yourself first.

Liberating boldness

ON TWO OCCASIONS in my forty-two years of life, it has felt like I've seriously lost the ground beneath my feet and seemed too small to deal with my circumstances. They felt bigger than me. Reading the Prologue, you will have learnt about the first occasion. The second time it happened was a decade later, while this book was in the making.

Here's how my ground disappeared: at what was supposed to only be a precautionary medical check-up, I received the information that my son, five years old at the time, had had a large hole in his heart ever since birth and needed to undergo traditional heart surgery. It was the experience of an abyss beneath me, in a split second replacing the world that I knew and that suddenly ceased to exist. It invited me to confront myself on very deep levels.

A fair part of that abyss kept coming back; I felt it beneath me every time I reminded myself that the surgery was getting closer. In what seemed to be a tension of my mind between wishing to simply flee from this situation and then also wishing to remain put and paralysed in front of it, I consciously reminded myself that this abyss was fictional. And life was here to be lived and trusted. And that's when the bigger, bolder, next level of me stood up.

This book is not about my personal stories; still, the point is that I cannot separate them from my leadership development. And you can't either. None of us can separate our leadership development from our experience of personal events, especially those that challenge the way we make meaning of our world.

That's because leadership is not just about what we do in the workplace. It is about who we are and how we make sense of the world. And then it is also about who we need to become to deal with everything that our life, our reality, our context offers to us as our work. The work in this sense means everything that is in front of us and waiting for us to do it, perform it, create it.

This is what the realm of leadership called ***Self*** is really all about – what the next level of you is, that's needed for the performance of the next level of your work.

The coaching process is a wonderful opportunity to explore this. And there is something important we need to distinguish between leaders' motivations for entering this space. Some leaders start coaching because they are searching for concrete solutions through direct advice for the current issues in their leadership that have become too overwhelming for them. Others do it because they perceive personal learning and exploration as a process that holds transformative power for themselves and their leadership. They know they'll have to change for things to change. And they'll have to find their own answer to *how*.

That leaves the former often being disappointed by the coaching process, simply because they are reluctant to understand this learning process as their own responsibility for a vulnerable journey into their own desires and their own comfort zones that go against those desires. This is a journey in which their willingness to change themselves, and explore how to, plays the major role.

This makes leadership in the realm of ***Self*** also extremely confronting and uncomfortable. Here's why: as leaders, we have to be continuously conscious of what we really want in this world and then also aware of our own patterns of being and doing, our own assumptions and illusions that cause us to stand in our own way. We have to constantly question what actually serves us and our realities, and what serves our worlds through us. It is a process that never really ends because it is a process of growth that is never really completed for any of us.

What we bring to that process is a number of our worlds and realities: inner, outer, business, family, relationship, friendship, many often overpacked ones that are very hard to navigate, let alone serve or find deep, fulfilling meaning in. And yet, it's possible to learn how to successfully serve all these realities once we accept the possibility that our identity that we have constructed may be too small for what we need to do, and that the majority of our leadership development work will be just about that – becoming a new bigger, bolder identity.

That is why by developing leaders, we are performing a most profound task of developing better humans. We do not evolve as leaders without evolving and becoming better people ourselves. And without evolving as persons, we can hardly find meaning in life, especially in those abyss-opening moments, those challenges that otherwise remain utterly inexplicable to us because we cannot find meaningful reasons as to why they have happened to us.

We often start our search for meaning out of two reasons: either our life has become so painful or it has become so dull. Once we recover, not many of us continue confronting ourselves on the self-exploration journey. I like to think that the bold leaders do.

Bold leaders create meaning. That is the value they add to their worlds. We cannot create meaning for our teams, families or communities if we are unwilling to continuously search for it ourselves. And, as human beings, growth is where we eventually find it; all we need to do is look for it. True leaders have a hunger for learning in all circumstances. Because they have an insatiable hunger for meaning.

There is something most bold in our choice to accept the practice of learning as a way of living and leading in all circumstances. I had a client, an engineer, who was a very down-to-earth leader. In every one of our coaching sessions, we would travel together across different parts of his reality through a series of metaphors. I don't think I've ever had the privilege of coaching anyone else who was ready to go to such personal depths. And when I acknowledged him for this commitment, he said readily: "It helps me to make sense of life."

There was something liberating and bold in this leader's attitude. He seemed to be ready to defy good and bad life circumstances and the persistence of many serving and damaging self-images by always, always uncovering new meaning at the deeper level of everything, of his entire inner and outer world. Confronting his current self in the service of creating the next level one.

I'm tempted to say that his attitude sounds wiser than life. But I dare to know how it feels. It feels like a liberating boldness – this ability to always and again re-create yourself to do your work in the world.

CHAPTER 1:
Hunger for Learning

I HAVE NOTICED two issues when working with some leaders in the area of their personal development: either they are sporadically committed to the process or they are – what I call – superficially involved in it.

As a consequence of either of these approaches, I have rarely seen their personal development create a profound, lasting change for them or help them shape their unique and destined contribution to their teams and organisations, their worlds.

Intentionality and commitment play a key role in leaders' approach to their leadership development. The way they dare to learn with clear intentions to explore themselves and the way they keep doing it continuously has an impact on how conscious, creative and effective their leadership becomes.

It has an impact on the development of their leadership consciousness that eventually supports or prevents any truly daring change of their teams, organisations, or any systems these leaders belong to.

Bold leaders understand the transformative power of being a learner in their life and leadership. Not only do they welcome the learning, they have a hunger for it.

Here's what I believe about that hunger: when evolving leadership consciousness becomes a collective hunger, the world will stop starving for prosperity. My vision is that we choose to hold this hunger as our key leadership priority in the service of healing the world.

Personal leadership development

I'd like to clarify the meaning of some important concepts related to growing leaders: personal development, leadership development and their intertwined relationship.

Personal development is a process of deepening self-awareness and expanding one's identity by exploring one's own developmental edges and continuously going beyond them over the course of one's life. As such, it is an adaptive challenge rather than a technical one.[14] Let's compare them in order to understand them better.

The solution to a technical challenge is learning a new skill and applying existing know-how to solve the problem. An adaptive challenge is connected to the way we make meaning of our reality. Unlike a technical one, it can only be met by shifting one's mindset: upgrading one's internal operating system in order to increase one's level of consciousness and expand one's identity. Metaphorically speaking, we resolve a technical problem by adding a new tool to our toolbox. We resolve an adaptive challenge by expanding the size of the box.

Since personal development implies the questioning of our reality and the expansion of the meaning we attribute to it, it is an adaptive challenge. As such, it is often difficult and edgy, evokes resistance, takes time, has no clear path or rules and its intended outcome is one's mind-shift.

As for leadership development, probably one of the most important misconceptions among leaders who venture into their development journey is that the change they are looking to experience will be of a technical nature. In other words, they expect to learn a few new skills to help them better manage their complex business realities. There are – at least – two issues there. First, the complexity of their world is such that it can hardly be managed but rather navigated until we actually learn to create from it; and second, a few new skills won't do the job. What leaders really need is a different level of consciousness through which they will be able to experience their complex realities differently.

Ronald Heifetz, one of the world's foremost authorities on the practice and teaching of leadership, spoke about adaptive challenge specifically in the leadership development process. Although many issues in that process, as he says, appear bundled, meaning they are partially technical and partially adaptive, many leadership development efforts fail because we approach them as a technical challenge instead of what they by their very nature mostly are – an adaptive one.[15]

It is important to understand that when we fail to see leadership development as essentially an adaptive personal challenge, our efforts to develop leaders are in fact unsuccessful. One of the reasons we fall into this trap is because of our human nature that wishes to solve challenges with existing know-how and fairly quicky. Another skill and we've grown a leader! A half-day workshop and we've got it! Make it quick and painless! Yet, in reality, developing leaders is a complex adaptive challenge to which we do not and cannot have a clear solution. The complexity of the process matches the complexity of a leader as a human being.

What's essential in this development process is a leader's commitment to be all-in. Here's why: in an adaptive challenge, we are simply part of the problem and also of the solution if we are ready and willing to take ownership of that concept and be accountable for our own change.

That's why all the coaches and leadership development professionals can only help to develop leaders, but they cannot actually develop them without their own willingness to change themselves. That's also why all coaches and leadership development professionals believe that people are naturally creative, resourceful and whole[16], and as such they've got all their answers within.

When embarking on a coaching and development journey, leaders must know that there's no one coming to rescue them, only to lend them a helping hand while they're attempting to rescue themselves from the mindset that no longer serves them for their leadership work.

Now let's see how adaptive and technical challenges co-exist in the overall leadership development process through the inner and outer game of leadership.[17] In addition to these two games, there are also three domains of leadership effectiveness – processes, competencies and consciousness.[18] It's important to understand how the games and the domains fit together so as to be able to understand what leadership development really includes or at least to differentiate between developing leaders and perhaps developing managers.

The leadership processes and leadership competencies belong to the outer game of leadership. Processes are the domain of management and they help leaders with effective use of resources enabling the successful business. In their essence, they represent a technical challenge. Competencies are visible in leaders' behaviours and are correlated with their leadership effectiveness. They can represent both technical and adaptive challenge. The technical challenge of acquiring an additional skill or the adaptive one of changing your assumptions that drive your behaviours, even though different in nature, can both actually impact your leadership competencies as they result in your different behaviour.

And here we come to the core: leadership consciousness is the inner game of leadership. It is leaders' inner operating system, their beliefs and assumptions, the way they are making meaning of the world based on which they make decisions and act.

Changing the inner operating system is an adaptive challenge. There's no additional tool or few-step solution to help leaders shift their mindset unless they are open to shift the way they make meaning of the world, to expand the tool box, to go beyond the edge of who they think they are and how they make sense of their reality. To evolve their consciousness so that they can become the one they could be, but are not yet in this very moment. The next level self.

This inner game of leadership consciousness directly impacts the outer game of leadership competencies visible in our behaviours. In fact, it drives it. That's why any true attempt to grow leaders starts right here – in their consciousness. A land far too complex to be resolved by a quick few-step solution. Evolving our consciousness is an adaptive challenge and an essential part of leadership development.

Although mastering the entire leadership game includes mastering technical challenges as well, by focusing on them only or mostly, we could help to develop a great manager, but we would not develop a leader. Because the inner leadership game impacts the outer leadership game, there is no effective leadership development without personal development. In order to develop a leader, we need to include the development of a person, a human being, in terms of developing their consciousness as a fundamental step to mastering the entire leadership game.

Personal development and leadership development need to be seen as intertwined challenges. Let's call this challenge personal leadership development. This challenge needs to be accompanied by the leaders' commitment to go deep under the surface, their willingness to remain in the enquiry of their leadership. It also needs to be approached as a disciplined practice, if we wish to see effective development.

This book, in its essence, is about personal leadership development. Let's start unpacking what that is within the SOUL framework.

The daring upgrade

Bold leadership starts with continuous openness to learn from ourselves, others and the world around us. That is what takes leaders to their higher consciousness, after it has first taken them deeper into themselves.

Here's one of the quotes that best promotes the imperative of leaders as learners: "In a time of drastic change, it is the learners who inherit the future. The learned usually find themselves beautifully equipped to live in a world that no longer exists."[19]

The thing is, times of drastic change in our world are never-ending. In fact, they are the regular nature of our world. We often hear that a highly complex setting we live in represents the context that requires fundamentally different leadership capacities than those traditionally developed in once successful managers.

I'm not sure we can pinpoint that moment in time when the world became more complex to require different leading capacities, but that's irrelevant. What's more important is to understand that changes really happen constantly, until the point that we just acknowledge them as our reality.

Encouraging leaders to accept the perspective that effective leading is conscious, continuous learning is their essential strength in the face of the current and any future complexity. Because if they don't want to remain equipped for what no longer exists, they must take the system upgrade imperative seriously.

Let's pause for a moment to explain what we mean by these two terms: complexity and the system upgrade.

To understand complexity, we need to notice that complicated and complex are two different concepts requiring a different approach. While we can use the help of experts to support us in figuring out the solution to complicated problems, in complexity we are faced with completely different rules, which makes it impossible for us to predict the right answer or a solution. Complex is uncertain and unpredictable.

It is the land in which there is a lot of what we don't know and we also have no reference point to those things we don't know. Given the fact that one of the basic human needs is safety and certainty, complexity is in fact a land of discomfort because it requires us to start operating from a level yet unknown to us.

Operating from an unknown level

A client had been recently promoted to the leader's role. It was how she was rewarded after years of successfully executing tasks as a team member, functioning independently, working hard, keeping things under control, and minimising any possibility of mistakes.

I asked her how she was, just to open up our first coaching conversation, and she went straight in, saying: "This is beyond my control. I am in over my head."

This is how she introduced me to the discomfort of her reality which was obviously somewhat more complex than she had been expecting or even felt equipped to deal with. What I thought was very good about it was that she'd obviously reached the point at which she was ready to admit it and speak about it.

"There are moments when I feel I'm going to give up everything. There is simply too much being asked of me."

"And what do you understand is being asked from you?" I wanted to make sure we both knew what we were talking about.

"Everything!" she exclaimed and went on to explain how she needed to make sure that the day-to-day work went smoothly, on top of creating a vision for the market, and empowering her team to pursue it. And these were only the requirements of her professional role, which seemed to be taking most of her day, most of her life. Those belonging to her private life were just occasionally mentioned here and there as she attempted to squeeze them into her overpacked business reality.

At that moment she made it sound as if she still held her team member role, on top of which she had just been given the leadership one. She made it clearly sound as if it was about working more and pushing harder.

Six months into our coaching relationship, and she started to open up to the fact that it was really about working in a different way. So, when I asked her what she was beginning to realise about what was really expected from her as a leader, this is what she answered this time: "Well, there is still a lot on my plate every day, but I've redefined a few important terms in my leadership vocabulary."

"Such as?"

"Such as that having responsibility for something does not necessarily mean being in control of the final outcome. Such as that taking care of the people in my team does not necessarily mean being responsible for their emotions, and confronting someone does not mean getting into personal conflict." And then she smiled before she added a really big change at the end: "Well, even asking for help is not a sign of being incompetent."

"Oh," I said, "that sounds like a big change."

"I'm not saying I'm fully there though," she said, quick with her disclaimer, "but I'm starting to get it. I've seriously started to get it."

"And what does it give you?" I asked, curious.

"Confidence," she said. "It gives me much needed confidence." "And you know what," she proudly added, "it gives me courage."

What this story tells us is that this client was really learning and starting to operate from a different level; metaphorically speaking, this was from the upgraded system equipped to run her new circumstances as if they were more advanced applications. And this system was downloadable and installable through her personal leadership development, her coaching and learning process.

So, what is this system and its upgrade? In simple terms, this system is framed in our consciousness that determines the way we make sense of our reality and our circumstances, and then has us make decisions, think, act and perform accordingly.

When the level of our performance is not up to the level of what our reality expects of us, we won't solve it by working harder even though this is exactly what we may automatically start seeing as a solution. What I mean by working harder, is working more but in the same way, which may even help to re-establish a sense of safety, control, or whatever gives us comfort at first. But in the current complexity of the leadership world, this is a choice that will eventually lead to an exhausting struggle rather than a sustainable solution.

Rather than working harder, the mismatch between the levels of our performance and the demands of our reality can be more sustainably solved by working differently. And to be able to work differently, we need to make sense of our reality in a different way. For that we need a different, higher level of consciousness. We need to restructure the current one and structure a new one. We need to upgrade our operating system to get to the new level of our identity, our next level self.

The journey that goes from our current self to our next level self, the one which involves upgrading our operating system, holds many edges for us to cross. Our current self is faced with an edge and invited to cross it by our next level self. These are moments of extreme discomfort in which we are likely to feel threatened, frightened and even shocked.[20]

The path to this higher level of consciousness goes through the painful depths of our comfort zones, but there's really no other way to upgrade our operating system, and transform the way we make sense of ourself, others and our world.

And that also is the only long-term solution leaders ever manage to achieve, because they won't manage to have the context's complexity downgraded, no matter how patiently they wait for this to happen. They are deceiving themselves with this illusion.

We wait to have more time, we wait until our work has become more routine, until we have completed some projects first, hired more capable team members this time, etc. These are all illusions in the world that is in a constant state of change, because even if you feel you've reached what you've been waiting for in one moment, you are just about to realise that in the next one the status has changed once again. And then again, and again, and again.

Your deep personal learning is a never-ending imperative because the change in the world around you is your never-ending reality. You learn as long as you lead and the more intentionally and committedly you do it, the more effective your leadership is likely to be. The bolder you will be on all your next levels, and there will be many of them.

What makes a difference to your success in the process, is the way you as a leader dare to learn.

Facing the complexity of ourselves and our reality requires leaders to take their leadership development seriously. And some leaders don't dare to develop other than learning skills and techniques within the outer game of leadership.

Whatever their choice is, they have their right to it. As a result, many of them will continue as great managers, not leaders, because leadership takes deeper developmental work. It requires us to boldly shift our focus to the inside game of leadership.

Shifting our focus from our outer world to our inner world is what takes us off the surface and straight to our core, straight to our soul. The place where we restructure the old version of our identity just to be structuring back our new bolder self. This process requires everyone to take a serious approach to their personal learning. There are no exceptions. Absolutely none.

And some leaders will continue to consider themselves exceptions, convincing themselves that they can still be effective even if they skip the requirement of the personal learning process. They need to be reminded that nothing reduces the possibility of innovation more than a conservative, fixed know-it-all-so-I-don't-need-it attitude. There is not one field where you could not always learn more, including yourself. There is nothing to which you could not go deeper, if you dared.

Leadership development that has true transformative power is a daring upgrade imperative, a bigger, bolder game. Nothing less than that.

The how

How we upgrade our operating system is a very legitimate question. I will answer it from two perspectives. The first one refers to the powerful developmental tool leaders use and the second one to the leaders' learning attitude.

As previously mentioned, much of my work as well as my own personal leadership development is inspired and informed by the Universal Model of Leadership™. This model is best brought to life through the Leadership Circle Profile™ 360-degree assessment tool.[21]

For the last few years, I've been supporting my executive clients in diving deep into their Leadership Circle Profile™ (LCP) results to understand what they bring as leaders and how this intention of theirs is perceived and experienced by their environment.

Seeing themselves through this tool is an opportunity for them to start an adventure and "pursue becoming all they are capable of being – growing in self-awareness, wisdom, knowledge, and insight".[22] Those who find credibility in measurement will be glad to know that this pursuit is in fact measurable through the LCP leadership competency called Personal Learner, a part of the Self-Awareness dimension.[23]

In addition to the point of measurement, LCP not only offers a range of key leadership competencies, but they are also presented in the context of leadership effectiveness and business performance by being either correlated or inversely correlated to these two elements.

The fact that the LCP dimensions are put in correlation with leadership effectiveness and the business performance index enables leaders to understand how their assessment results relate to their leadership brand in their business reality, in terms of their behaviours that have the most impact on how they are perceived as leaders.

Additionally, these correlations help leaders understand the true importance of single competencies. For instance, the Personal Learner competency has a correlation of 0.80 to leadership effectiveness.[24] For the sake of comparison, the Decisiveness competency that stands for the leader's ability to make serious, tough and timely decisions also has a correlation of 0.80 to leadership effectiveness.

Despite leaders being much more likely to be worried about how they score on their decision-making ability, in terms of the impact on their leadership effectiveness, these two things seem to be equally important: how well leaders develop their ability to make decisions and how much they are ready to be personal learners. I find this to be a very interesting piece of data in support of the practice of learning.

Even though LCP stands for a credible source of information about your impact as a leader, this tool is much more than the measurement of your leadership. It's a doorway into your deep developmental work. I've witnessed that for many of my clients it is a powerful experience with deep insights and huge emotional impact.

LCP invites leaders to open up a vulnerable conversation, one that they have probably never had before. And as such, it brings immediate change.

This conversation poses questions around how much of their leadership is purpose-led and bold and how much of it is in fact fear-driven and small. And that is the conversation that not only pulls leaders to the next level of their thinking, but also clearly generates the *how* of their operating system upgrade.

This is the transformative depth and power of LCP.

The second perspective refers to your learning attitude. In Organisation and Relationship Systems Coaching, we use the term metaskills – an attitude, stance, philosophy or "come from place" that leaders stand in by choice in their leadership.[25]

The first metaskill leaders need to stand in by choice to be able to learn is boldness. Every change starts by confronting self, and there are many selves we provide home to. Confronting all those that we know, and those we are yet to meet, requires boldness.

Then it's commitment, simply because there is no point in time that we can call the end of the learning journey. There is no final destination, only numerous stops that require us to make numerous decisions while staying committed to one key choice: to learn and to grow in service of our next level self and our next level work.

In addition to boldness and commitment, there are another two essential metaskills that leaders need to adopt when being personal learners. These are curiosity and humility.

Leaders as learners are curious about themselves and open to listen to the dynamics they create with the world around them. Even when they "know" something, they ask, "What other truth co-exists together with my own, right now, right here?" Curiosity equips them to search for meaning and saves them from remaining equipped for something that no longer serves them because it's long gone. Curiosity helps leaders realise the opportunity that arises as their current level reality starts disappearing in front of the emerging one. If they miss that moment of opportunity, they've missed the essence of leadership.

And finally, humility. Humility stands for a certain liberation from the ego. We can define it as a metaskill that enables us to objectively observe ourselves, through the response from others and therefore our impact, through what we are strong and also what we are weak at. We recognise it by seeing leaders move their focus from the importance of their status to what is really important for them to learn in order to do their work.

I've recently found a true inspiration for the process of learning in the fascinating poem by Amanda Gorman, the US youth poet laureate who read her words on the occasion of US President Biden and Vice President Harris's inauguration. While she was referring to the nation, her poem can address the development of any human being: we learn not because we are "broken but simply unfinished" in our state of becoming; and by learning we do not attempt to become "perfect", but rather "with purpose".[26]

And that's how we arrive at the question of purpose. There is no leadership without purpose. Purpose is what we uncover in the land of enquiry, which is a metaphor I use to indicate serious learning about ourselves, our relationship to others and our world and a deep exploration of what really matters to us.

Those leaders who truly dare to learn will not only step into this land, but will make the land of enquiry their never-ending leadership practice.

The why

While there is a general belief that it would be easier to lead with the right answers, leadership is much more about staying with the right questions while acting on one's purpose in the larger context of the world. The questions about one's *why*. Those questions require leaders to be in a state of constant enquiry of their life and leadership, connected to their very souls to search for the meaning.

I still remember an episode from one of the most transformative leadership training programmes I've experienced so far. There were three questions written in the middle of the white flipchart paper: Who are you? Where are you going? Why are you going there?

I remember looking at those questions and reading them over and over again. I didn't even attempt to answer them, as I was too occupied with taking in this insight: I have never ever asked myself these questions.

I've been through some challenging personal and professional experiences through which I grew, but I've never really hit the pause button and asked myself these questions. Could it really be that I had failed to stop for just a moment in my life so far to stay with these questions?

In that particular moment I had a direct experience of what it means to be too busy doing life to live it meaningfully instead. When this happens you don't actually know where you're going or have a vision of where you wish to arrive. Those questions truly started my self-seeking journey and, in time, I have reshaped them in the way I felt was needed.

Facing these questions will inevitably make everyone feel vulnerable. Some people will take a deep dive into this reflective conversation with themselves. Others may stay on the surface, well protected by their own judgement about these questions, when in fact we cannot miss reflecting on them over and over again as we will otherwise fail to explore the very essence of our leadership.

These questions support the deepest process of maturing our leadership. Even though they are presented in the realm of ***Self***, bringing our leadership to life through the SOUL framework will pull us to revisit this land of enquiry over and over again, taking us deeper each time into the questions that live in it.

Let's explore these questions the way I see them: What am I here for? Where am I going? Who am I being along the way? How am I acting on my path?

What am I here for?
In other words: What is, in fact, the purpose of me being in this world?

Leadership development begins with meeting our own purpose. That's our reference point to everything else. Some will call it our North Star, the layers of which we continue discovering in the course of our life.

Meeting our own purpose is a disciplined practice of listening to what our soul desires, to what truly matters to us when liberated from the protective shackles of our ego, from the fear. It eventually means honouring our own responsibility to express ourselves from the very core of our being in doing our work in the world.

Expressing ourselves from our purpose, from what holds most meaning to us, from our very soul, gives us this raw boldness that our deep transformation requires. Anderson and Adams speak about "the staying power required to transform ourselves and our organisations in spite of the vulnerability of change, the political risks, the self-doubt, the fear and the possibility of failure".[27]

Notice the term "staying power". I imagine it to be a process of building an inner capacity that allows us to stay with a huge discomfort and enables us to be fearless on our deepest spiritual level at our most important moments, our moments of transformation. I believe that building that capacity depends on whether we welcome the practice of seeking, of constant enquiry, whether we dare to keep asking ourselves what we are here for. Or, contrary to that, failing to build it if we consistently and judgementally run away from those questions.

More than once in many corporate realities where task execution is prioritised both over purposeful achievement and a connecting relationship to others and oneself, I've heard this question being labelled as something philosophical, esoteric, abstract, something absolutely not practical, and as such not meeting the demands of the leaders' reality. Knowing that this is a starting point of true leadership, it's very sad to hear such a perspective.

I imagine that it can be uncomfortable because it often requires moments of complete nakedness of our identity. And that, I can understand, is hard to welcome. But it is in that place that we meet our boldness by realising what matters most, what our work in this life is and because it is our work, the one we are here for, it is worth all our risk. If we do not dare to explore the essential question of what we are here for, we will be expensively charged with both missed potential and lost fulfilment.

On the other hand, staying with an enquiry to get to know what is worth our risk will provide us with an almost unshakeable capacity, an unimaginable boldness to face tangible, concrete, down-to-earth challenges that we know so well in our reality. Because once we tap into our purpose and choose the risk of leading on purpose, the dimensions of our boldness are almost unimaginable. All the right doors open, things make sense, even hardship has its meaning. Doesn't it seem like a fair enough life deal?

So, what happens if we don't do that? Many people remain stuck in their life-long internal conflict because of not having taken the risk to do what was most important for them – the risk of who they must be or what they must do at their deepest soul level.

There are many leaders leading in business, health, education, politics or acting in many other institutions of public life and shaping their individual as much as our collective world right from the place of this internal conflict. What that does is, it leaves us all with the world full of people who did not dare to choose what makes them come alive. There's a good chance that they have never even dared to ask, never even dared to seek. We need to be conscious about how it actually feels to live in such a world.

The second important question to ask ourselves in our own land of enquiry is: ***Where am I going?***

The essence of this question is our vision. To really know where we are going, we need to have a vision of what that actual place looks like rather than the path towards it. Because the path can, as it happens, be modified many times along the way. Exploring this question allows us to shape our vision of the future, the place where we're going in our life and our leadership.

It is our task as leaders to start uncovering our purpose to find out why we are here in the first place. Once we know our purpose, it becomes our leadership responsibility to translate it into the future vision. Having a vision means taking the reason why we exist seriously.

Leaders dare to have a vision of what is theirs to bring to the world and to create out of the place of their purpose. The truth is that vision normally does not come overnight and especially if we fail to engage ourselves in the enquiry of it. But even if we do, sometimes we are not absolutely clear about where we are going, but we do feel pulled in a certain direction. It's important that we consciously and intentionally stay committed to this pull. It only means we're in the important process of clarifying how our purpose can be translated into the vision of our tangible and meaningful future reality.

The third and perhaps the most vulnerable question is: ***Who am I being along the way?***

The moment we start realising what our purpose is, what our work is, we need to ask ourselves this question. Because what we are really after is to discover if who we are is big enough for what we desire to do out of our purpose. And then also, what we need to change about ourselves to be able to carry on our important work in the world.

So, how do we actually look at who we are?

Many leaders have a firm image of who they are, until they don't because it's challenged in one way or another by experiencing some sort of a rejection or failure. As sarcastic as this may sound, this really is a moment of celebration of your identity, this feeling as if you've just disappeared from the face of earth when in fact you've only been created. If not before, the true self-exploration usually starts in this moment.

This exploration of who we are is also very much seen through the lens of any relationships we're in, which helps us see the range of who we are and who we can be as we ask: Who am I and who else can I be in relation to different people, things, events, even emotions? And then another important question connected to our range: When I am being that way, what's really my impact? What's really my leadership influence?

Knowing who they're being along the way determines the way leaders shape and achieve their vision. In its essence this process is about exploring their own inner assumptions that create their self-image that has potential limitations to achieving their future vision.

This exploration merges with the exploration in the next question of how I am acting on my path. This is because these same or other assumptions, in addition to shaping our self-image, also drive our behaviours that potentially limit our current capacity to lead our future vision.

And so, finally, the fourth question: ***How am I acting on my path?***

This question has a lot to do with consciously, intentionally and boldly moving forward to lead with our vision of tomorrow – today.

If the vision is a picture of the future reality, in order to get there, leaders need to be doing today what fits the picture of tomorrow. What can stand in their way of doing that, is themselves along with their behaviours.

It is essential that we all stay conscious of the fact that whatever way we are acting in our daily life brings us closer to or further away from our vision.

And what often happens is that, instead of daring to lead with their vision, leaders willingly succumb to the pressure of having their decisions be very tactical in the service of resolving daily obstacles rather than building the road towards the future prize.

Leaders are often very much concerned with managing their complex realities, until they start understanding two important things here. First, their realities cannot be managed but only navigated. Second, the actual requirement in front of them is to not only navigate their realities, but also create in the midst of their unpredictable nature. To shape and lead with the vision that most matters to them. With full confidence. Right into the unknown. Straight through discomfort.

This is again the conversation around our operating system that needs an upgrade for us to be able to act on our path in such a way that will take us closer and not further away from our vision. The level of consciousness will increase and not limit our capacity for this work, with our bigger identity, our bolder self that is up to the task.

Leadership is not guaranteed to anyone by either their formal authority or their personal traits. What stands between the possibility of being a leader and the reality of being one is *how* and *when* leaders act.

Leaders act on the work that needs to be done; they don't merely nurture a secret desire about it. From this perspective, the essence of leadership is action as a result of enquiry and deep awareness.

And so, as a leader, you are responsible for asking yourself continuously and consciously about the way you are acting on your path. You are responsible for how, by acting on your path, you are shaping your current and future reality. You are responsible ***for*** your reality. You are responsible ***for*** your world.

The aim of these statements is not to give you a leader-as-a-hero perspective but rather to empower and enrol you as a leader in any context.

In this chapter, I've spoken about the hunger for learning that can take leaders to their higher consciousness, after it has first taken them deeper into their enquiry. What this also means is that before they reach the heights of their self-empowerment, they'll have to first dare to hit the lows and enrol in a deep, painful self-disruption.

Your reflection

Here are a few questions to reflect on:

1. What are you here for? Where are you going? Who are you being along the way? How are you acting along your path?

2. What are you still not daring to learn? What's comfortable in that? What's not?

3. What else requires you to pause and reflect?

CHAPTER 2: The Art of Self-disruption

WE UNDERSTAND THE world through our own stories, which are in fact assumptions that we call truths. We, as leaders, are invited to constantly disrupt them.

Our assumptions represent the way we see the world being made up and help us to live and lead in our realities. Until they don't, which is when we are forced to confront them.

We all experience such moments in our life. These are the moments we are called to a painful process of disrupting ourselves simply because we stand in our own way of successfully performing our leadership work. We experience them, but don't necessarily welcome them.

When we do, we're able to travel to the next level of consciousness at which our world, including our truths about it, once again makes sense and we are able to bring effective leadership to it.

A lot of leadership development is breaking through the frame of our assumptions. It's a process that feels most unsafe. Coaches and leadership development professionals often use less invasive terms to indicate that a disruption in self has started: an insight or an aha moment. What that really stands for is the moment in which what you've believed to be one of your fundamental truths is suddenly simply – destroyed.

The dictionary offers the meaning of the verb to disrupt as to drastically alter or destroy the structure of something. In the personal leadership development context, it means altering or destroying the structure of what you believe at the identity level and really the structure of who you are.

Letting go of what you've believed to be the truth for as long as you have been aware of yourself is not easy. It is hugely uncomfortable, to say the least. It is an invitation for all possible protection mechanisms in us to start sending alarm sounds about the seriousness of the situation, its hazard.

I'd like to normalise the fact that it is confronting and it is scary. And you'll reap the fruits of it. But there is no way you can truly experience self-disruption, and remain well protected from its discomfort. Please, for the sake of your bigger self, give up this idea.

The image of a bold leader is often associated with confrontation of other people. They are seen as leaders who have the ability to stand up and confront others. I'd like to change or add, if you like, an important piece to that perception: bold leaders have the readiness to fearlessly confront themselves first in service of their own development.

Bold leaders are ready to break through the frame of their own truths that no longer serve them even though they may still very much feel that they keep them safe. They know that if they neglect to do it, they will not become big enough for the work they need to do in the larger context of their world.

To picture the magnitude of the discomfort of self-disruption, we need to say that it is not felt only cognitively. It is an uncomfortable feeling on the body level as well. When we are confronted with the invitation to let go of the assumptions that we see as protective to our safety, our entire body protests. From the loudness of this protest, we get to understand the importance of this assumption in terms of the level of safety it provides for our entire being.

To tap into our leadership boldness, we need to dare to tap into our assumptions first. There is a video I first saw years ago, while I still was working in the corporate world. The title of the video is "Dare"[28] and while it is an advertisement for clothes, it really sends a message that we do not need to step back, when we are actually capable of boldly stepping forward.

It was amazing to listen to the powerful tune of Vivaldi's "Summer" from *Four Seasons* and watch how the main character's daring capacity literally turns her fears into dust. It's hard to watch that without feeling an invitation to step up or step forward. Certainly not back.

"Dare" was sent to me by a female colleague who must have clearly noticed how I kept myself imprisoned by my own stories of safety, while there was boldness waiting just outside the frame of those assumptions that I called truths. A frame I refused to think was breakable. Fears I refused to imagine could turn into dust.

As a leader, you need to simply welcome the perspective that any story frame is breakable. Any of our fundamental truths are changeable. Any fear is reduceable to little unimportant particles. It's bold and it's possible. Is it comfortable? No. Is it terrifying? Yes. Is it inviting? Thinking of the final prize of your development work, what would you say?

And what do you feel would be possible for you if you allowed yourself to accept this invitation?

Cracking the code

I believe that, no matter how much importance we give to the process of figuring things out, we take some of the best and most important decisions in life in a fraction of a second and based on a number of intelligence centres in us other than our heads.

As much as it sounds confronting for some, we can't understand everything we do, nor do we even need to, with our head intelligence. There are many other places of knowing in us such as our body, our emotions, or our spiritual intelligence, indicating that we also think with our spirits, our visions, our hopes, our sense of meaning and value (SQ).[29]

Cracking the code is a metaphor for having something figured out. We can be quite unsuccessful in the attempt to crack the code of our leadership, if we limit ourselves only to our head intelligence. A true breakthrough requires more than that. It requires a beautiful self-disruption from which our heads usually try to protect us.

How do I crack the code?

"I get this, but how do I crack the code?" one of my clients used to say every time she faced her own resistance to an emerging insight. Cracking the code was her metaphor for her own change that she imagined to be happening almost in isolation from herself, a process which would require her to engage her head far more than her heart, if at all. It sounded like an invitation to a somewhat safe rational transformation rather than a whole-being transformation.

"How DO you crack the code?" I returned the question right back at her and that caused irritation on her side. "That's what I'm asking you. I don't know. If I did I would do it."

"And if we imagined just for a single moment, almost theoretically, that there was a part of you that knows? Somewhere in your inner world, there's a knowing about what exactly it takes for you to crack that code. What's that part of you and what does it know?" I continued, being compassionately firm.

Her eyes went teary as she struggled to keep a distance from what was beginning to be beautifully disrupted in herself.

As my work is predominantly in the corporate arena, more often than not I am meeting such head-centred leaders. Leadership Circle Profile™[30] describes them as reactively protecting themselves because they are keeping themselves safe through their brilliant intellect, seeking truth by remaining in their heads and providing rational explanations for it from a safe distance. Vulnerability is what truly shakes the ground beneath their feet and disrupts their meaning-making of the world. They tend to stay away from it.

What applies to every leader and is particularly relevant for the head-centred ones is the idea that leadership development does not solely happen in or through the space above our neck. Your knowing does not sit in your head only. In fact, a great deal of cracking the code is understanding just this in the first place.

The true art of self-disruption is to involve the many intelligences we possess. In my own development process, I've got to know numerous approaches that have resonated with me. Some were leading me to open up to my head, heart and guts intelligence centres[31], some were inviting me to see my body as my brain by cultivating my innate somatic intelligence[32], others to explore the wisdom of relationship systems intelligence (RSI)[33] that supports the capacity of any group of people to move beyond the personal to a powerfully generative collective identity, and yet others to understand spiritual intelligence (SQ) as what helps us put our life including our actions in the wider context of meaning.[34]

You'll do your own research into what could inspire you and make sense for you in your world. Don't forget to go beyond what you currently believe is rational. Have in mind that once you move away from your head as a safe shore, the journey of cracking the code will inevitably be a vulnerable, but successful and highly rewarding process. And there's no way you can sail through it without welcoming a disruption in yourself as a whole.

When the mind shifts, the change is not only cognitive. The change of you, the growth of you, cannot happen in non-messy isolation from your whole self. Welcome it as such and you'll be welcoming a new bold(er) identity.

Illusionary safety

In our personal leadership development process, we are inevitably called forth to disarm the illusions we have been nurturing and organising our identity around. As awareness is the prerequisite to any change, before disarming them in the process of self-disruption, leaders need to face their own illusions to understand how they truly play out in their leadership while they are being deceptively exchanged for truths. To that end, often within the coaching process, we ask leaders: Do these illusions serve you or not? Do they serve your work? And then also this: If they make you feel safe, what's the real cost of that safety?

We all have our own versions, names and stories behind our carefully nurtured illusions. Here I'd like to offer the top five that to varying extents I've seen repeatedly appearing in many of the leaders I've been working with. In the service of authenticity and vulnerability, I'll describe them here through the image of my own insatiable demons that exist in my self-constructed world. I'll also show the impact these demons have had on my leadership. Meet my five illusions to see how they potentially resemble your own.

Meet my illusions

The illusion of control: I'm worthy and safe if I'm in charge and in control. The long-term impact of this illusion is that most of the time it suffocates true passion and joyful engagement for the work.

The illusion of perfection: I'm worthy and safe if I'm doing things perfectly so I can triumph over others and therefore deserve to belong to the group. The long-term impact of this illusion is that most of the time it diminishes creation, authentic expression and purposeful innovation.

The illusion of knowing: I'm worthy and safe if I'm superior to others and their thinking and therefore self-sufficient. The long-term impact of this illusion is that most of the time it prevents true human connection and collective spirit.

The illusion of approval: I'm worthy and safe if the people that matter to me like and accept my choices. The long-term impact of this illusion is that most of the time it negatively affects my authenticity and integrity.

The illusion of all illusions, the one that puts them all together – safety: I'm completely safe if I'm in charge, deliver perfect results, know all the answers, and if those that matter to me approve everything I bring. The long-term impact of this illusion is that most of the time it negatively affects my boldness to step up and step forward.

Whenever my world operates smoothly according to these illusions, they provide me with pleasure and satisfaction in all the senses of safety and worthiness that they may generate on a short-term basis. The thing is that no world can operate smoothly for long based on these illusions, simply because they are illusions that can never truly be in place. They are unreal and unreachable. They are not the truth or at a minimum not the entire truth. And if one's world does seem to operate smoothly based on these illusions, that's just as the words say – seemingly so – thanks to their deceptive effect. In the long run, living and leading based on these illusions creates an impact that could not be further away from what bold leadership truly stands for, or a fulfilling life for that matter.

The illusions are nothing more than huge assumptions created from our experience. We create them to enable us to manage our reality, but they are eventually counterproductive. Being attached to them will disable us from successfully navigating the increasingly complex reality in our life and work. Then we'll be desperate to crack the code.

We'll start wondering why something happens to us and how to quickly solve the undesired reality. Solving our reality requires us to understand it in terms of raising our awareness about it. To understand our reality, we need to understand our illusions.

Because cracking the code means cracking our illusions. One of the very simple and most liberating life philosophies that I've learnt is this one: "Life itself is one big game that's all made up".[35] If that is true, if life is really all made up then we, as well, are all made up by ourselves. When cracking the code, what we actually need to crack is just that: our own image of ourselves in the world we're looking at through our own illusionary made-up frame. Why? To do what's next for us.

Is it just me, or are you also seeing this as an opportunity?

The choice of disarming illusions

The effect that the illusions as assumptions provide for us speaks to our basic human ego needs which we naturally cannot deny. The act of disarming these illusions, however, is not to deny our needs. It is rather to consciously accept the illusions for what they truly are instead of holding on to them for what we need them to be so that we can experience the pleasure of safety and worthiness.

While deceptively exchanging these illusions for truths may help us gain self-worth, acceptance and personal safety, they in fact take away much of our bold leadership potential. In the corporate world, I've seen many managers or formal leaders standing in their own way of becoming true leaders who are bold to bring more of their natural leadership to the world. When leaders start disarming their illusions, they actually start getting out of their own way to create a true leadership impact.

Helping my clients to do this work, I often apply the approach that views this process as overturning your immune system. This is the Immunity to Change method developed by Harvard University researchers Robert Kegan and Lisa Laskow Lahey. Kegan and Lahey talk about the immune system we all have and that is held in place and heavily supported by our big assumptions.[36] These assumptions are in the background of what they call our hidden commitments that prevent us from change even when we claim we're committed to it. We declare ourselves committed to something that we desperately protect ourselves from at the same time. This concept in reality operates as a perfectly oiled immune system, unconsciously preventing us from growing into our changed self.

To make this immune system easier to understand, let me share one of such huge assumptions that has been operating at the back of my mind, probably since my formative years and certainly throughout the period of my corporate career and beyond: people who ask for help are lazy and incapable.

That sounds very harsh, I know. As my world got more and more complex, I also very clearly realised that holding this assumption is not very intelligent either. And yet I'm aware that it goes hand in hand with me holding the illusion of knowing, being worthy and safe if I'm self-sufficient and superior to others and their thinking. Seeing the world through this lens, how probable is it that I'll be asking for help? And never asking for help, how likely is it that I'll be encouraging the spirit of togetherness, connection and success through collaboration? And yet, for years I craved trusting, empowering and inspiring collaborative connections in my professional life. A goal confronted with my hidden commitment: be superiorly self-sufficient and never depend on anyone for help.

By revealing those big assumptions or as I call them here illusions, we can see our unconscious commitments, and reach the point of becoming consciously immune to change. In this moment a self-disruption can begin by consciously releasing what we have so far believed to be the truth so that we can construct a different meaning-making of our reality, the one that is higher consciousness based. A different story through which we make sense of the world and the way we live and lead in it.

When leaders reach the point of revealing their big assumptions, they – as always – have a choice. They can choose to opt out of disrupting themselves and disarming their illusions, and they will continue to cancel their own impact in what otherwise could have been their true creative and highly effective leadership. They will make a decision to continue seeing themselves, others and the world *through* their assumptions rather than looking *at* them to create a more spacious frame through which to see their realities. Their own illusions will have them stay deceptively safe and away from self-disruption that is an essential leadership development process. Or they can choose to dive right into the discomfort, for the sake of transformation. In service of their true bold leadership.

Here's what I believe: true leaders choose unsafe. They choose uncontrollable, imperfect and uncertain. They choose all of that to crack the code of their own leadership. That choice cannot be made by staying within the existing frame of their brilliantly knowing intellect, or approval-seeking heart or triumph-hungry will. That choice can only be made by their readiness to restructure this frame, these safety-giving parts of themselves.

And the reason why they choose that is this: for the sake of doing their purpose-based work that is more important than the risk of their uncomfortable self-restructuring.

They engage their raw boldness to magnificently disrupt themselves to their very bones, just to be able to overcome themselves – make themselves up again and have their next selves meet their world at the next exciting level of complexity.

Your reflection

Here are a few questions to reflect on:

1. What's your most fundamental truth, the one that does not serve you?
2. What are the key assumptions you hold about yourself?
   If you let go of them, where would that take you?
3. What else requires you to pause and reflect?

CHAPTER 3: **Becoming**

PERSONAL LEADERSHIP DEVELOPMENT is the work done from the inside out, exploring one's own depths first. In that process, we get to meet different parts of ourselves safely tucked up in our illusions, our beliefs, our stories. The more we are ready to open up to these different parts, many of which could also be our wounds figuratively speaking, the more we will overcome our pain and become ready to create new value for our world. That's what our next level identity is that serves the world.

We disrupt ourselves; we explore ourselves; we heal ourselves, just to be able to meet our world with our new bigger, bolder story. It's the story of someone who is not only ready, but eager to create, to do their work in their world, to do the work to create change while being on purpose.

We may have started as what we call a victim - someone who felt they had insurmountable issues that were happening to them. The development process helps us overcome the victim image, and prepares us for the leader's role in which we act on purpose towards our vision.

Notice the journey that goes from being a victim, through an overcomer and to a creator. It's the process of who we are becoming for the work we have to do.

I'll speak more about leaders' work to create change later in this book. For now, let me highlight this conviction: if, in the course of the personal leadership development process, our leadership profile does not transform from a victim to an overcomer and then to a creator, we need to ask ourselves where we have actually missed unlocking our full leadership potential.

Simply put, this is where in the process we have remained locked in our selfishness to just sort out the current discomfort of our leadership role instead of becoming open to our true leadership service to the world. It's where we have not deeply explored and accepted our old story, owned a new one and then moved on boldly to create value through our work.

Let's now look at a couple of different concepts that can help us do that.

The first is a concept of our range and our stories. Let's define range as all the parts of ourselves: those we like and those we struggle to accept, those we'd love others to experience and those we're (un)skilfully hiding. Our range includes our light and our shadow parts, and our development helps us know them and eventually accept them both. Unless we accept them both, we will miss the opportunity to be empowered by them, to become strong and whole in what we label as our full potential.

In the previous chapter I spoke about the stories, or the assumptions that we call truths to help us give meaning to our reality. This chapter includes the conversation about our old and our new story, or in other words our past image, our identity that no longer serves us, and the new one we are becoming.

In that sense our old and our new story are much about our permission to first accept our entire range and only then exchange our own past image that lives in our old story for a new bigger one that belongs to our new bolder story.

With no acceptance of everything that we are and everything that we can be, there's no new story. We remain stuck in the old one that limits our work.

The second concept is our leadership impact, which is how we start creating legacy when we fully own our bolder new self-image. From that self-image we consciously and intentionally use all of our parts, all of our range with which we influence our world and create our impact.

Once we start eagerly owning our new story, we start adding new value to our world. We're no longer spectators, bystanders, silent observers. We are in the process of becoming creators of the contribution in our world, which is in my view pretty synonymous with actually becoming leaders.

Notice I'm saying becoming. That's because even when your old story becomes your new one, the process of growth continues with many other following new stories waiting in line for your further development.

Accepting your old story

Let me tell you a personal story about how I gave myself permission to accept my old challenging story, transforming it into a powerful new one.

Often in my life, I've felt the internal conflict between the part of me that opens up important tough conversations, the one that's a bold truth teller anchored in her integrity, and another part of me, the one that needs to be reasonable and politically savvy in order to belong to whatever group of people I'm in.

For a long period and especially throughout my corporate career, I consciously prioritised the latter, and the former would then wildly come alive with every denial of mine. The more I refused to accept myself as someone who brings the hard truth and names the elephant in the room, the more this quality was present in almost any of my circumstances. The more I was cornering myself into silence, the louder I would become. The more my environment was rejecting it, the less I accepted that part of myself.

Naming the elephant in the room

I remember still today how a ten-year-old me was rejected for not being willing to beat around the bush. We were in 4th grade and our final year with the loving teacher we'd had since we started at primary school. A group of girls got together to agree on the farewell present the entire class were to buy for our teacher. We had two options and we couldn't agree on the final choice.

Oh, and what if she doesn't like the option we go for? Some were worried more than others about making a mistake. And then suddenly one of the girls came up with the idea of consulting our teacher to help us decide. The rules of the game were set – we absolutely wouldn't tell her who the present was for and we wouldn't fully uncover what the actual options were. The outcome we were desiring was to get an answer from her on what would be the right choice.

The conversation with our teacher started. And as it went on it got more and more complex and further away from both the truth and the desired outcome. The elephant in the room grew bigger with every second of it. A balloon was inflated to the point of popping if only there was someone to poke it.

And that someone was – me. In just one instant I raised my voice and cut to the chase by saying: "Now, this is what we're actually trying to do here..." Imagine the looks I collected from the other girls in that very moment! I can still taste the bitterness of judgement and ultimately rejection. "Oh you, you had to say it and now you've spoilt everything!" the girls were hissing at me. "That was not a nice thing to do," my otherwise loving teacher said in a rather cold voice as she showed sympathy for their anger.

In fact, we did get the answer we were looking for. And the teacher eventually got the present she liked better. And I got the lesson. I walked to the school toilets to let that lesson sink in while I shed many tears and judged the part of me that just got me rejected from the tribe. The voice in my head went on and on, shaming me: Again? Really? Why can't you just comply? You'll never fit in. What's wrong with you?

So really, what was wrong with me then and in the many years afterwards while I – as you can imagine – so naturally continued to name the elephants I met in the many rooms I'd step into?

Fast forward some thirty years from that bitter-tasting event and I found myself in my own leadership development course where the course leaders named this challenge I was experiencing.

Naming is a powerful tool. It brings clarity to many painful issues and in that way almost instantly decreases their intensity. My leadership development trainers named many things on that occasion. They named the stillness, the edginess and the discomfort that fills the room when what shows up is the bold part of a leader that refuses to stay silent. They explained why people might shift in their seat, being at the receiving end of that boldness. That hard-loving truth. The one from a place of love but still fierce rather than soft. Truth that does not dance around but cuts right through. No partial integrity. A naked straightforwardness.

They also mentioned how this directness increases the sense of trust and safety among those shifting in their seat and feeling slightly uncomfortable. That's because they know that no important topic will be avoided[37] and the hard truth will be told in a straightforward, calm way and from the heart.

They named my challenge and, more importantly, they offered a context in which it was possible for me to perceive it as a gift through an intentional use.

A ten-year-old me who could not fit in because she could not keep her mouth shut suddenly became part of my old story. The story that tried to force me to silence myself in the face of what was not aligned with my integrity only so that I did not experience rejection. The story that has followed me ever since like a shadow consistently nurturing a conflict within me.

What I learnt then was how to embrace that part of me in my new story and bring it to my world. What I learnt as well about the ten-year-old me is that, in addition to giving herself permission to speak, she also had to take responsibility for the impact she had been creating while naming the elephant in the room.

In that sense, my trainers pointed me towards calibrating the *how* – or the way I'm saying something and creating impact – and not the *what* – or the core meaning of my message generated from my values. They encouraged me to continue telling the truth, they taught me how to best convey my true intentions while doing it, and they helped me find my value-based reasons to handle what looked like people's resistance to my voice and rejection of it.

That made it possible for me to accept my old story, and consciously and intentionally make space for a new one in which my integrity was at peace and my leadership was of service.

In terms of my range, it enabled me to accept blunt directness as an essential part of myself. Leadership Circle Profile™[38] calls it Courageous Authenticity[39]. It's a creative leadership dimension assessing leaders' readiness to take tough stands and initiate tough conversations that are being avoided by others.

Courageous authenticity, in fact, measures the courage of leaders expressed by how authentically and directly they are dealing with risky issues in the workplace. It may be a somewhat controversial dimension that the world does not easily welcome, but let me tell you this: I have not come across any leader, not one, that has not shown traits of worry when seeing low scores on their Courageous Authenticity dimension. Not a single one.

In the executive coaching and leadership development work that I do today, courageous authenticity is one of the key things I get hired for. I get paid by my clients for not dancing around but rather voicing the truth I dare to know about and for them. I don't have to be right but I do dare to know the truth that comes from a place of love and I voice it in the most respectful manner. Even when it's fierce. Especially when it's fierce.

Often, I feel it is a potential risk for me and I witness that it is hard for them. Still, in the long run, I refuse to withdraw. They shift in their seats and they also soak in the sense of trust as I invite them to have a conversation they have never had before. Because transformational conversations are both rarely comfortable and endlessly needed.

To be able to do this work I consider important, I've learnt to calibrate my impact, so people around me feel safe in the company of my voice and I feel at their service. The work we now committedly do together changes me, changes them and changes our worlds.

So, do your work to face and then accept what you consider to be difficult parts of yourself that belong to your old story. Sometimes the more difficult they are, the more important they will prove to be. Transform them into your new story because they are likely to be the source of your most influential leadership.

In the leadership development context, revealing and accepting your old story through the process of self-awareness liberates the space for the next one. The new one. The one that eventually liberates ***you***. The one that unleashes your own leadership and prepares you for what your next level work really is in the world.

Own a new story

Until we are ready to fully own our new story, we are limiting our own impact and our influence in our world.

We cannot hold two Self versions, keeping the previous version of ourselves and stepping into our next level. This is a conversation about the choice we have with our stories: we can shrink into the old one or we can expand within the new one. Our impact will eventually tell.

I used to have a very limiting idea of what impact is. I was perceiving it only through the leaders' responsibility to calibrate *how* they are acting so as to more intentionally influence the experience others may have of them and their behaviour.

For instance, I'm aware that in my own range, my blunt directness that can serve me so powerfully can at times also go to the level of rudeness, which happens if I'm not taking responsibility for my impact. So, it's important for me to keep being intentional about how my blunt directness comes across to those at the receiving end.

While this definition of impact is immensely important, I've also come to understand the meaning and importance of impact in a much broader sense than that. I see leaders' overall impact as their legacy, their contribution, the added value they create in all its tangible and intangible nature.

I see leaders' impact as their non-formal authority. It is an empowering impact, coming not necessarily from a formal position of power, with which leaders enrol others in what their vision is for their teams, organisations, communities, for their worlds.

With every new story you dare to own about yourself as a leader, you are expanding your leadership potential for making a greater impact. For bringing the best of your new story, the best of your bolder leadership through your passion, your dedication, your expression, your creation.

That is a bigger meaning of impact. Taking responsibility for that impact means taking responsibility for everything that you're creating and as such expressing in your world.

Taking responsibility for that impact means taking responsibility for bringing your whole leadership to your world.

Next level Self

Leading is creating. We create from the moment we are alive. We create from ourselves and our stories; we create from others and their stories, from our world and our collective stories. We constantly create something, because the real work of leaders is to create.

In the realm of ***Self***, what we create is the next level of ourselves as leaders. And so, the real reason why we get to know ourselves in this space is only to be able to get over ourselves.

Getting over ourselves, we build a bigger, bolder version of Self, but again not to construct a self-centred leader. We do it to grow empowered leaders prepared to contribute to their worlds with their elevated potential.

Many leaders get stuck in their victim stories and as such never unlock their full potential. That seems fairly obvious. Equally, but perhaps less obviously, many leaders start their development journeys and become attached to their overcomer role along the way.

That means that they may have survived challenging situations, gone deep down to explore themselves, and then never dared to create anything that's bigger than them. And while the process of self-development is a never-ending one, its true purpose is not to become both the means to an end and an end itself. The self-development process is not your work; it is your support process for doing your leadership work in your world.

Truly bold leaders understand that they've got their meaningful work to do. Exploring their Self helps them find out what that work is and what their next level Self is that's required for that work to be done.

So, this is the beginning of the journey. There are many other important areas this book will take you to; there are other essential realms of leadership. A usual course of our development may be that after we've explored the relationship with Self, we sense an expanded capacity to explore our relationship with others as the next essential step in our leadership journey.

Once we understand that leadership is about creating what matters most to us for our worlds, we also begin to understand that everything that really matters, anything that's larger than us, is created together.

Every single thing that has the potential to be larger than us is created together with other people in radical human connection, a concept that requires us to journey into our hearts to experience its meaning more profoundly.

While travelling the road from ***Self*** to **Other**, perhaps we'll perceive it to be the one that the Native American teacher Phil Lane describes in these words: "The longest road you will ever walk is the sacred journey from your head to your heart."[40]

Let's begin now. Boldly.

Your reflection

Here are a few questions to reflect on:

1. What is your old story waiting to be let go of? What's the new one coming in?

2. What is your leadership work that has just started revealing itself to you?

3. What else requires you to pause and reflect?

Before proceeding to Part 2, here's an invitation for you:

Great leaders are personal learners. Those that know how to upgrade their individual or collective operating system have a competitive advantage.

Visit www.boldleadership-culture.com and schedule a strategy call with me to discuss how to apply **Leadership Circle Profile™ and Collective Leadership Assessment™**[41] in your organisation.

PART 2
OTHER

Leadership is radical connection.

Where leadership lives

One of the ways to deeply understand what leadership is, is to explore where leadership lives – where it happens and how it shows up. As much as it starts with ***Self***, leadership does not live in self-isolation. Leadership is very much the process of growing together in the realm of ***Other***, which requires everyone to bring their radical humanity and raw human magnificence to the table. Leadership lives in radical connection.

To explain what our leadership as radical connection means, let me start by describing what our connection usually looks like in reality. We usually respond to each other by reacting *at* each other. We react at what other people are, do or think; we react at what they bring. Our instant reaction is not to create from what others bring, but rather to vote if we agree with it or we don't. If we see them as adequate or inadequate. Rather than being radically connected, such an approach makes us humanly judgemental. Rather than seeing raw human magnificence in others, we vote about whether we like them or not. And the radical leadership approach in the realm of ***Other*** is to always look for the wisdom in another human being, the impact of which makes us both wiser.

My work includes a variety of what I consider to be very inspiring committed roles. They include coaching, training, mentoring, speaking, writing. I love them all. Still, there is one of them that I find most resonant and thrilling every single time I'm doing it. It's my role as a coach trainer. I've wondered at a certain point what it is that makes this particular role so fulfilling for me. Who is it that I'm being, what is it that I'm doing when I'm in this coaching training space that inspires me and inspires others as together we feel encouraged to show up fully? And as I imagine myself literally stepping into that space with other people, I envisage walking through an immensely deep connection that fills our entire universe. There is a key human ability we all so naturally feel as we venture into that space: our ability to see into each other and see ourselves in one another. That makes our connection radical. Let me put the volume up on radical connection and say: it makes our human souls joyful and free as they fall in love with each other's expression.

I realised already some time ago that the greatest skill of a coach is their presence. Presence does the work. If you are ready to embrace this, you'll quickly understand that presence really does all the work in simply anything we do. And presence is just a short term for indicating that we *see the other, hear the other,* are fully *with the other* and recognise ourselves completely *in the other* human being.

Taking this concept to the corporate arena, what I'm realising from almost all the coaching sessions I have with leaders or their teams and especially in times of Covid-19 pandemic lockdown, is that such a presence of leaders (or absence for that matter) is noticed and essential. It leaves others feeling empowered and optimistic or simply worried and alone.

This is because presence is a radical connection with the other person. As I'm training new coaches, I allow myself to model this capacity of the human soul to its fullest. And I've never ever completed one single coaching training job without asking myself what our world would look like if we allowed ourselves to be radically connected at all times: to see the other person, hear them, be fully with them in all their range of emotions and, while being at the receiving end of their intended or unintended impact, recognise ourselves in absolutely everything they bring. Absolutely everything: both shame and glory. Instead of just judging them, or voting for whether we like them or not. Now, that is ultimately radical.

To think that way would also radically expose us. If nothing else, it would expose us in front of ourselves as we dared to walk out of our shelters that carry the name: "I'm worse than" or "I'm better than". That would radically expose us and be a risk, at least in the face of our own image. But leadership is not safe. Risk is exactly what leadership is all about. Leadership lives in exposure. To lead is to be exposed.

Trying to stay safe is equal to trying to play small. As Marianne Williamson said: "Your playing small does not serve the world" and "There's nothing enlightened about shrinking so that other people won't feel insecure around you".[42] As a matter of fact, as we shrink, we might be more likely to invite other people to shrink too, so together we deprive the world of our joint greatness instead of – as Williamson would add – our presence automatically liberating others as we are liberated from our own fear. As leaders, it is our soul mission to bring ourselves and others alive. Let's not betray this mission by shrinking and being small for each other.

Because no matter how small, in true leadership we can never be safe. There is nothing safe about leadership. Safe leadership is a lie. Instead of being safe, leadership is a joint vulnerable growing process. Leaders grow as they lead and together with those they lead. It is a space of not knowing. And not knowing it together. It's the process of including others in all the uncertainty that matters to you as you're holding a vision that it may matter to them too. Because it matters for the world that you imagine to be a great home for your humanity.

How likely are you to be wronged and judged and fail in your leadership? Oh, very much so because, as I have said already, it is human nature to constantly vote for or against whatever is brought to the table. Regardless of that or just because of that, let it always be your radical humanity and raw magnificence that you bring rather than a small, illusionary, safe version of yourself in your leadership. While there will surely be at least some who will find the former to be world-changing and inspiring, there will certainly be no one including yourself who will feel any inspiration about the latter.

And that brings us to yet another belief around the place in which leadership lives. Leadership lives in a hard-loving truth.

Much of leadership is opening up the conversation that we know is needed. Many of the conversations that we know are needed feel most uncomfortable. And yet they are a priceless gift: open, spacious, and relationship-oriented conversations that are not as much about giving the right answers as they are about asking the important questions. These are conversations that set the context for the transformation of everyone involved.

So, what makes these conversations so needed and uncomfortable at the same time? There is a very short and straightforward answer to this question: the truth. Whose truth? Everyone's. There is no more important conversation than the one in which everyone shares their truth.

The truth we share in these conversations is the one about each other's unintended impact. We're calling each other forth to our individual and collective brilliance and out of the safe cave. It's a hard-loving truth we offer with integrity and compassion and receive with much gratitude.

At the same time, it's a vision we're holding for each other and for us together. True leadership plays a major role in naming the gap between the current reality of who we are and how we act and the vision of our future being and acting. It is the gap that we speak out loudly and boldly to each other from a place of love, encouraging each other to close it.

In such conversations people hear each other, see each other, experience each other and accept each other. They truly welcome each other. Rather than being super ready for those conversations, leaders simply take the leap because they will hardly ever feel absolutely ready for something that is so vulnerable, exposing and risky. Instead of making sure they've got all the right answers, leaders are simply being bold enough to bring the hard-loving truth. It is how they bring their leadership in the service of growing (with) the other. Because leadership only truly lives in relationship with others.

As it does so, leadership in itself is an act of genuine care – caring for the other and for what we co-create together. It's also an act of loving confrontation as we bring heart and radical openness to each other.

If, so far, the leadership in the realm of ***Other*** has sounded like an intangible concept, know that it has its very specific components. They are leadership competencies that each leader must develop to ensure the effectiveness of their leadership: caring for others, encouraging teamwork, cooperation, mentoring and development and interpersonal intelligence as the ability to understand and interact with others. Leadership Circle Profile[43] altogether calls them the Relating leadership dimension and they are described, together with their impact, in a very down-to-earth manner.[44]

As much as they can be clearly understandable by one's head, I'm not convinced they can ever be completely comprehended unless leaders engage their hearts in the leadership of others to be able to live, work and function with them from a place of love, and not a place of judgement.

It is with their hearts only that they are able to grasp the ultimate meaning of leadership of others: it is a space of trust in which we lean into each other with the fullest expression of our unique magnificence, with the very same human aspects that we all have, just demonstrated through somewhat different personal life stories.

CHAPTER 4: Seeing Me

LEADING THE OTHER changes us both. It is an act of radical humanity, a dance with the other in which, rather than becoming masters of steps, we become explorers of the depths of our trust and connection. We willingly accept the risk of erasing the line between leading and being led as moments require. We're prepared to be strong, humble, dare to know, dare to be wrong, accept each other's flaws and invite one another's brilliance. We are ready to undoubtedly believe in each other's potential.

If this does not resemble your experience of leading others, the truth is that you have probably, instead of leaning into another to the extent that truly bold leadership requires you to, chosen the deceptively safe distance.

By doing so, you've deprived yourself of the possibility of one important leadership dimension that the Co-Active Leadership Model calls Leader Beside that leads *from* the other.[45] When we don't lead from the other, we eliminate the opportunity to help empower leadership in everyone. But what does it mean to lead *from* the other and how do you do that? I hope the rest of this section will give you some answers to the *how*, as long as you remember the true meaning of leadership from the other. It's the meaning of the radical connection as a come-from philosophy in approaching the other human being. Leading from that place changes every individual and every relationship.

Thich Nhat Hanh would tell you that we are here to awaken from the illusion of separateness.[46] And leading the other in the way that changes us both could probably be the first sign of our eyes opening.

Reflection of me

What I see in you is what I've got in me. Depending on whether we are seeing what we like and approve of or the opposite of it, this can be the easiest as well as the hardest leadership concept to digest.

At the beginning of the coaching relationship with my clients, I usually ask this question: Who inspires you and what for? Once they've come up with either well-known people or persons from their close surroundings and named the inspiring qualities that they see in them, I point them to the idea of they themselves owning these qualities as well. The very same qualities exist in them or else they would not have been able to recognise them.

As I do that, I can see their world and their identity expanding in front of their eyes. They've just become a little bit bigger at the idea of possessing courage, boldness, wisdom, huge heart or whatever there is that inspires them most. Their world has suddenly become one of many possibilities as they look at their heroes and see their own reflection in them.

And even if they are not yet convinced and are still questioning it, if there is not a clear acceptance of that yet, there is for sure no real resistance to it either. There may be a little hesitation teamed up with some shyness as they embrace the next questions with genuine curiosity: Where does that quality show up in me? Where do I bring it in my life? Where do I need to?

While their face shines at these enquiries, you can sit back and watch them being open to experience. I've noticed that in such moments little is required of a coach apart from holding space for the client who does all of the work. And the work is the act of staying with the inspiration that the other human being evokes in them and perceiving those inspiring qualities as their own inner worth.

Owning that inspiration instantly brings people to act on it. It's a place of fulfilment that makes everything not only possible but also so very inviting. It's easy to deepen the conversation from this place: Where else would you like to bring this quality into your life? What would be possible for you? What difference would it make for you, for the people around you, for your world? Through these questions, they are gradually building their own sense of empowerment. And we as coaches, we as leaders, are supporting them with humility in that noble task of nurturing their own brilliance and boldness.

What really happens there is that, suddenly, what started as an inspiration in another becomes an inspiration in oneself. What I see in you is what I've got in me. That which you bring is what I accept. Not only do I accept it, but I also welcome it and choose to lead from it, choose to find wisdom in it serving my own leadership. What perhaps could have been a confusing term of "leading from the other" makes so much sense now to them as a concept that gives joy and creates empowerment. It fosters deep listening to, seeing and appreciating the other. If we went a bit more practical and tangible at this point, we could call it a truly engaging and genuine team play. A heart-based collaboration.

What fundamentally happens here is that we trust the potential of the other, and as we're inviting more of it, we are also becoming more ready to recognise it in ourselves and bring it out to the benefit of both and beyond.

Imagine yourself looking at everyone you interact with through such eyes. Imagine allowing everyone the opportunity to inspire you. And just before your head has dropped the idea, know that it's not as much about their ability to do so as it is about your choice to allow your heart to look for it.

I agree that this choice is harder to make once we travel throughout the full range of other people, there where the colours become a bit darker. Rather than being curious explorers, in a split second we become angry fighters against what's hard to accept in others and almost impossible to imagine as also living in ourselves. It's normal. It's human. And as leaders we need to know that this also represents a moment when we actually fail to lead from the dimension of other and we need to know that we can do better. We can learn how to. And for the impact of our leadership, it's important that we do.

Impatient for your flaws

It's in our human nature to have parts of ourselves that we consider flawed and that we therefore try hard to reject. Then, suddenly, we get faced with others who dare to expose those same parts so openly. They dare what we don't.

This is the moment we react: I'm not giving permission to myself to show up fully here and I'm equally not giving it to you. We're not in love with each other's expression. I don't really want to see into you because I constantly see you as a reminder of something that I'm trying to forget that exists in me.

Notice how the idea of "what I see in you is what I've got in me" lands somewhat differently in this context. Still, I point my clients towards exploring how these same qualities exist in them simply because they have been able to spot them. And that speaks of their importance. This time their whole-being response does not seem to create an expanding and fulfilling energy, but rather one of cold rejection. At least, at first.

Rejecting you, rejecting me...

"Excuse me, but that's nonsense. I'm not saying I'm perfect but I do my share of the work! She's irresponsible. She does not care. She obviously has other priorities. People have to work harder to cover up for her missed deadlines. I have to work harder because she does not deliver what's expected from her."

She went on and on with her story. Venting her anger. Vomiting her fury. Her annoyance was partially a reaction to my initial question: "What aspect of her reminds you of you?"

When she had voiced out loud all that she needed to say, she held her breath for a tiny little second before she shouted: "How dare she? How DARE she?"

"What exactly does she dare?" I asked.

She paused as if clarifying her own thoughts. "She dares..." and then another moment, "she dares to prioritise other things." Now, already speaking with her voice significantly calmer: "And she seems to do it with such resilience, as if it doesn't upset her at all."

"What are you aware of now?"

"Nothing," she replied as her calmness transformed into a cold sharp voice. It sounded as if she had got closer to understanding the dynamics that was happening between them, when she chose to stop and go back to her anger. Staying with anger was easier than facing something else.

"I'm aware of the fact that she is irresponsible and lazy. That she's incompetent. And that this level of dedication and this lack of ambition won't get her anywhere. Nowhere! Ever!"

"And what does that leave you with right now?"

"It leaves me with a problem. I've got a problem and it's her. She is my problem!"

"You really are angry with her," I reflected back as my client was crying frustrated and helpless tears. "I am," she said almost with relief, "I am."

"What's this anger really about?" I asked her as I saw something started to shift in her.

"You know," she said as she looked upwards almost as if searching through her own thoughts that wouldn't go away, "I would never dare to behave like that." And then she continued: "I'll never be able to understand people who...", and that's how we slowly, yet finally moved away from the woman in her story just to get closer to herself.

We don't accept the behaviour of others that we would never dare to have ourselves. That is why rejecting certain qualities in others is simply a sign that we need to come closer to exploring those same qualities in ourselves.

Our normal human reaction to other people's behaviour we do not approve of is to judge them and try to change them. And let me ask you one thing about the last time that you tried to change someone: How did it go? I dare to know that it wasn't the greatest success.

So perhaps we could explore a different path: the one that says that everything eventually takes us to ourselves. Because it's never about us, until it is. And it's much easier to accept that we share the same qualities with the other person, while we do not consider them to be flaws.

So, what do we do as leaders when we are faced with other people's imperfections? Rather than throwing those people under the bus, we remember the phrase: If I see it in you, I've got it in me. Encouraged by this thought, you're likely to see that you do not dare to welcome it in you just as equally as you are refusing to tolerate it in the other. I'm not trying to amnesty anyone for avoiding their responsibilities. I'm trying to make the point that everything – whatever we label it, good or bad – exists in all of us and it is subject to our choice when and where we bring it out. Because as Rumi says: "You are not a drop in the ocean. You are the entire ocean, in a drop."[47] Hopefully, you'll notice the compassion this attitude brings into the space: compassion towards yourself and the other.

There are many concepts I've learnt in my dedicated personal development. Some of them are complex, and some are really simple. They are so simple that it is even more significant and simply shocking how I discovered them only as I was approaching my forties. One such concept is self-compassion.

I had not discovered the true meaning of self-compassion until I learnt to differentiate it from self-pity and self-indulgence. Self-compassion is different from being immersed in your issues to the point of isolating yourself in a state of victimhood. It is equally different from taking the path of least resistance and eventually manipulating the challenges of the much-needed change in you.

Self-compassion is accepting your own humanity in times when you suffer or you feel inadequate, insecure or failing. Self-acceptance and self-compassion are therefore intertwined and the relationship between compassion and acceptance is no different. By having self-compassion and truly allowing yourself to be human, you will feel compassionate towards others and allow them as well to be what they really are – humans.

Compassion, however, does not mean letting self or others off the hook. If you went in that direction, please come back because compassion means coming from a place of love while we are not excusing others from their duties or responsibilities. It is not about excusing anyone, but rather accepting everyone for the human beings that they are. Having shared human experience and reflecting shared human aspects. Compassion is also an antidote to impatience for other people's flaws. If there's no compassion in leading others, judgement fills in the space.

Allowing space for compassion does not mean that there is no space for challenge. On the contrary. Reading through this section, you'll understand how and why.

Leadership of others is very much about compassionate challenge or what we could call supportive and loving confrontation. Use whatever terms work best for you, but learn their essence. And the essence of such an approach is that you hold the bigger vision for other people even when or in particular when their behaviour says that they can't see it themselves and you pull them to that vision through love and acceptance. Meanwhile, with full self-awareness, you see your own reflection in their human aspects, compassionately.

Oneness

I trust that, if not before, at least while reading the ***Self*** part of this book, you have realised the importance of accepting yourself as a whole. Welcoming your light and your shadow, the parts that cannot be separated, the ones that make the undividable you. The beginning of this section speaks about leadership in radical connection that changes both the one who leads and the one who's led as they recognise each other in one another along the way. Such a connection is the fundamentals of leadership. That's the root of all leadership inspiration. Unfortunately, it's the root we walk away from so easily despite the sufferings we consequently feel.

Because our world is organised in a way that promotes categories, classification, boxes, and whatever else seems to be labelling people's apparent differences rather than highlighting their commonalities, it seems we have convinced ourselves that connection is in fact an illusion. It is not. Separateness is.

We could go into deeper philosophical discussion about everything being an aspect of oneness. Still, I'd like to stay with what helps us on a practical level to come closer to the experience of oneness with each other amidst the world structures and the lifestyles that heavily support exactly the opposite. For that purpose, let me ask you this question: What's your truly important story? And as you attempt to answer it within you, ask yourself: When was the last time I shared it with someone? Anyone? Ever?

So, when was the last time you shared your story with those you lead? And have you asked them to tell you theirs?

Here's what I believe about the power of stories: if at least one third of all the talking we did was opening up conversations to share our personal stories, disconnection would hardly be an issue we face. And we would experience love, acceptance and compassion instead.

Inviting others into a real human conversational arena is a leadership mindset, much more than a communication skill. Freeing up the space for them to share their story and offering ours in exchange makes the commonality of our human experience so close and so clear to all of us.

Sharing the moments that shaped us, the thrills we had, the battles we fought, the joys and the pains we went through in our lives. Please walk away from the deceptive idea that this depends upon your mastery of good communication skills rather than being dependent on the bold steps you take in walking from your head to your heart.

Many leadership approaches will say that leaders need to build the capacity for storytelling as a tool with which they can address people's emotions in the first place. But the thing is, to address others' emotions, you have to offer your own. Your story needs to include you.

I believe that leaders as storytellers need to be ready to tell and hear those very personal stories, the ones that are challenging to share. To quote the American psychologist Carl Rogers, what is most personal is most universal. What is universal brings us together by reminding us that in all our appearance we are just an expression of our common humanity.

This is true leadership happening in radical connection and us, both leading and being led, ready to boldly claim: "I know you need to trust me to let me hear your story. But know that when I listen to your most personal challenges, I feel we are one in the way that we can appear in and experience reality. When I hear your story and you hear mine, we both wholeheartedly understand how we could so easily find a place into each other's reality."

And therefore, connection is not an illusion. Separateness is.

Connection leads to inspiration and empowerment. It leads to the people you lead feeling accountable for each other's good, for the common good, the good of the whole. In the organisational context, how hard are leaders trying to make their team members accountable? Engaged in caring for the good of the whole, whether that is their team or their entire organisation? Even though they may appear equally successful in the short term, there is a substantial difference between those organisations inhabited by single achievers driven by their individual interest and those who provide a home to people pulled into empowered action by caring about their shared identity and the common good.

A large amount of my own coaching practice is dedicated to organisation systems coaching. All too often the leaders of these systems approach me due to a lack of engagement among their people. All too often, once we start the work, we find out together that it is a lack of connection that leads to the difficulty in understanding and experiencing their shared identity, their one vision, their oneness. Whatever tools we use to create the desired outcomes, the most powerful path is opening up the conversation in which people dare to be radically human.

From that radically human space, people share their team's story and their own story that lives within it. They do it instead of resisting their connectedness, and hiding in the apparently safe separateness that leads to suffering disconnection from self and others. In such conversations it becomes blindingly obvious how the presence of a working-in-silos approach is merely an absence of connection and inclusion. Leadership happens in such conversations as both those leading and being led allow themselves to take in what the rational mind cannot fully grasp but the soul already knows.

As mentioned before, the Universal Model of Leadership™ and Leadership Circle Profile™[48] assessment tool will tell you that Relating[49] is an important dimension of the most desired creative leadership. It measures a leader's capability to relate to others in a way that brings out the best in people, groups and organisations. It's a very clear definition and a very welcomed dimension.

And yet, to make it real, it requires relating to be more than just a set of skills or tools. True relating is the mindset. Having a relating mindset means holding this leadership stake, this belief in both inspiring and frightening moments: Leadership happens in radical connection – a place where we can see into each other and see ourselves in one another.

Your reflection

Here are a few questions to reflect on:

1. What do you reject as a reflection of you in others?
2. What's the world like because of the way you're connecting to others?
3. What does it mean for you to be radically connected?
4. What else requires you to pause and reflect?

CHAPTER 5: Trusting

YOU COULD BE thinking now that seeing leadership as radical connection is possible or at least easier when there is trust. In that case, please consider this good news because trust is a choice.

I was once convinced that others to a large extent defined my capacity to trust. When my leadership matured, I learnt that I choose trust just as I may choose safe leadership. It is a matter of personal decision.

Another important differentiation that I came to understand about trust is that trust is what I call a three-folded dimension. We may be inclined to think of trust as something we primarily place in others but in fact there are two other places in which we choose to put and nurture our trust: in ourselves, in others and finally in whatever we know is bigger than us both regardless of how much it is beyond our rational understanding.

Your leadership effectiveness is heavily affected by each of the three layers of trust and I choose to speak about them through the lens of what I believe to be their respective impacts: integrity, intimacy and allowing.

Integrity

I have already spoken about the importance of integrity earlier in this book. It is my firm belief that if such a complex matter as leadership ever needs to be reduced to one thing only, that would be acting in integrity. In this chapter I wish to define integrity in the context of trusting oneself.

In its very essence, integrity in this context means holding the belief that I am enough. I am worthy, safe and loved as I am. Holding this belief is the sign of me trusting my own wholeness.

When you don't lead others from the place of trusting your own wholeness, your interactions with them always represent the validity test of your being and of your doing. Before you know it, this test becomes an insatiable search for approval sought from what we imagine to be others' authority. Leading others from the place of their approval of you suffocates your boldness and inevitably leads to conformity as a safe harbour. You in fact deprive yourself of your own inner authority that inexorably waits for your integrity to arise.

Contrary to that, when you do trust your own wholeness as a leader, others will likely see it as your self-confidence and it will inspire them to passionately support you and determinedly find their self-confidence in themselves too. Because self-confidence is charismatic. It's also cosy because it eventually diffuses the sense of safety among others. Confidence starts within, which is what the root of the very word and its meaning throughout time may suggest: have full trust or reliance in one's own powers and resources.

Trusting oneself is almost the same as holding the right to be oneself. When my clients receive results of their Leadership Circle Profile™[50]assessment, more often than not the most painful is to see the scores on the lower circle end. It's where their reactive leadership shows up, the one that has gifts to a certain extent, but is hugely detrimental to their leadership effectiveness if it is overly present. Reactive leadership consists of three dimensions: complying, protecting and controlling.[51] In my view, each of these dimensions respectively can tell a very powerful story about trust in oneself, others, and the universe through the lens of integrity, intimacy and allowing.

If complying takes too much space in a leader's profile, I dare to know that the assumptions they hold about their reality are preventing them from fully holding the right to be themselves. Their wholeness is not in place unless others give them permission to be so. Their trust in themselves is conditioned by other people's opinion about them. Pleasing others rather than honouring their own values, principles and visions they stand for makes it hard for others to trust them.

Notice that pleasing others and consciously relating to them are two essentially different things. While relating makes them a better leader, complying reduces their integrity. Complying leaders keep their integrity closeted by holding back who they are and what their creative expression is, largely because they do not trust themselves either. They don't have trust in their natural creativity, resourcefulness and wholeness in terms of being willing to risk their expression in the face of the potential judgement of others. Because they choose to hide their integrity, they make others blind to it.

I'm always curious to know what unlocks in my clients once we open up the conversation about them trusting themselves or others trusting them. I make sure they understand that, equally with leading themselves first, leadership starts with trusting themselves first. It is their trust in themselves reflected in their integrity-based leadership that inspires others to trust them. The true trust is given to them by others, because they genuinely trust themselves.

That is how our self-trust paves the way for our trustworthiness.

Intimacy

Radically close

"I can tell you about intimacy and leadership. Well, unless you ask me about the exact explanation of intimacy. You see, it's hard for me to define it. Still today, I haven't come up with the right words. Right in terms of deep enough, deep as the experience of intimacy I had in that training room. But if you ask me about the experience, I can easily recall it in my whole being still today. Right now, I can tell you about my sensory experience, sight, sound, touch...

"I can tell you about the feeling of being alive as I held others and was held by them. I can tell you about the sense of liberation as you face your fears with the weapon of trust. Oh, I can tell you about the feeling of trust – that deep, wide metaphorical container in which you willingly swim with another human being.

"In fact, I could tell you about the literal jumping from the heights into that imagined container held by the other person and feeling safer than ever. That's intimacy. Getting in touch with each other's humanity. Leaning into the depth of our connection, as if leaning into each other's souls."

She was looking at me as I said these words, slightly less against the idea of intimacy in leadership. Still hugely puzzled in her attempt to take in what she'd just heard. "I'm not sure I'm completely getting your explanation," she said politely.

"Oh, I'm sure you're not," I said to my client who was visibly wondering what on earth intimacy had to do with leadership. "You see, it's not about getting the explanation. It's about getting radically close to other people so you can get the experience."

Just like this client, I remember how I wasn't getting it either during my own training when they wrote the equation of trust on the big whiteboard before us, trying to explain what it means to get radically close to another human being. Trust was defined by the level of your credibility, reliability and intimacy, while being reciprocal with the level of your self-interest. It all made sense apart from the element of intimacy. It brought confusion and a certain discomfort. It was too strong a word, making me shift in my seat. Somehow, this word did not belong there.

Still, that leadership development programme was designed to have us experience intimacy defined as an essential leader's capacity before we would attach a different, probably more common definition to it. I'm sharing what eventually became my intimacy definition at the risk of failing to do justice to the actual powerful experience within the programme: intimacy is the depth of our connection experienced through unconditional presence, acceptance and safety.

Intimacy is much more about the truth than anything else. In that sense, I believe that the quote by American novelist Taylor Jenkins Reid summarises the essence of intimacy: "People think that intimacy is about sex. But intimacy is about truth. When you realise you can tell someone your truth, when you can show yourself to them, when you stand in front of them bare and their response is 'you're safe with me' – that's intimacy."[52]

Notice how intimacy suddenly becomes a discussion around your capacity to fully trust the other. Opening a conversation is an aspect of intimacy, especially opening up one that evokes discomfort.

Because it is about trust, intimacy is also connected to a very common topic from leaders' realities – that of feedback. I don't think I've ever completed a coaching relationship with a client without touching on the topic of giving feedback. They always wish to know the best way to communicate what they label as a negative piece of feedback. At the beginning I normalise their attempt to outsource their own accountability to me and collect a few safe steps for themselves to follow simply as a shield against their own discomfort in giving feedback. And then I point them in the direction of noticing their underlying intention to stay protected and distant from the other person as that person is receiving news that may be unpleasant and may not land well.

And the truth is, feedback is much more about our readiness for intimacy than our possession of good communication skills or collection of tips. In fact, I believe the best tip for giving feedback is to raise a leader's awareness about the importance of them being emotionally close to those they lead instead of protecting themselves by withdrawal. And that's also because withdrawal rarely comes alone. Quite often it is accompanied by judgement and people can feel it. And no one wants to feel as if they've been left alone and judged while receiving less pleasant news about themselves.

It is not distance but intimacy that truly guards both those who lead and those being led in the face of what may feel and sound vulnerable. Intimacy is deepening the relationship. Distance is deepening the pain.

Intimacy, for that matter, is as much about the ability to say as it is about the ability to hear. Saying comes through opening up the conversation. Hearing comes through listening to the other, listening to what they say and what they hold back, listening to their needs through that instead of hearing one's own assumptions about it. Distance and withdrawal are fond of assumptions. In fact, they keep generating as many assumptions as possible for leaders, while they remain well distant and therefore in the absence of anyone else around they could possibly check the truth with.

Distance, as opposed to intimacy, is how leaders establish an illusionary sense of safety in the absence of trust. Add criticism and arrogance to it and you'll get the reactive leadership dimension called Protecting[53] that in the long run does not do what its name suggests. It does not protect you, but rather puts your true leadership at risk, making it nothing but a safe lie.

Without intimacy leadership is transactional rather than relational. All head and no heart, to simplify the terms. I dare to say, in the long run, it has little meaning as well. The relational leadership, the one we bring intimacy to, is the one that's real, vulnerable and spacious.

Intimacy creates realness in our leadership and our leadership is as powerful as it is real. Real leadership is vulnerable. In fact, we take the position of distance just to avoid being vulnerable. In other words, to avoid admitting we don't know something, we don't know how to, we may need help, we are wrongly assuming that what being vulnerable really is, is being weak.

In the land of trust, being vulnerable simply means showing the real side of our humanness. And the power of that is visible in the inspiring connection it immediately creates. Many times, to recognise the importance of connection is to become bigger than our own discomfort and step into the land of vulnerability in the service of common good. As much as it looks scary, this is in fact a liberating step, the one that allows us to find the meaning of our human experiences together rather than enjoy the truly frightening disconnection.

It is also how, from realness and vulnerability, we arrive at spaciousness in leadership, an element that makes it an inspiring, bigger, bolder game. As deep and as meaningful as the collection of human experiences.

And so, rather than asking *how much* or *how to* trust others, I believe that leaders' work is to boldly explore first *what it is* to trust those they lead. What does it mean to *actually trust them*? How *real or vulnerable* are they or aren't they ready to be with those that they lead?

Answering these questions is likely to provide their leadership with all other answers they may need about *how to* actually do it.

Allowing

I wrote most of this book in 2020, the year that challenged us on so many levels. Apart from the world pandemic that reminded us how little control we generally really have as human beings on a global scale, I'm sure that there were a number of personal stories that felt even more directly challenging to our own illusion of control.

I was confronted with one such story relating to the health of my son. I mentioned it at the beginning of Part 1 of this book, in the context of our circumstances that sometimes feel much bigger than ourselves, thus inviting us to dive deep into our personal learning process and explore our growth edges.

The truth is, I was not the only one confronted with this story I'm calling mine here. My entire family was. My son was confronted with it as much as he was able to understand it at his current age. We were in it as a strong team or – to phrase it better – we were as much as we chose to be, as much as we chose to collectively trust.

It was a situation that called for the next level of each and every one of us as well as the next level of our family as a collective entity. It made me realise that if we put our trust in each other's presence, our joint dynamics and whatever we believed was bigger than us, we would be allowing much more miraculous outcomes to happen than we could ever have imagined to occur through our control.

Bigger than me

In September 2020, during a regular medical check-up, my five-year-old son was diagnosed with an atrial septal defect. It is a congenital heart defect in the septum between the heart's two upper chambers. The septum is a wall that separates the heart's left and right sides and this defect is usually called a "hole" in the heart.

"Your son has a large hole in his heart," is what she told me in the children's hospital that morning of the 7th of September 2020.

And she continued: "The large opening means that more blood than normal is pumped to the blood vessels in the lungs. Such children usually have no symptoms apart from a potential heart murmur. And in fact, if we hadn't diagnosed it now, he would probably be OK and able to live until thirty or forty years of age..."

At that point I lost her. I lost the clear sound of her voice. I couldn't breathe. I was unable to take care of my son Noa who was sitting next to me in that small room that suddenly became so suffocating. I couldn't even ask her to stop talking and I so much wanted her to just shut up. Shut. Up. And she kindly did when she became aware of my reaction to what she was saying.

She was so caring that she asked the nurse to help me recover from the shock and promised she would be back after a while to explain to me what is considered to be a common disorder that modern medicine can easily resolve.

I recovered in about twenty minutes. She came back. The moment she started talking, I lost her again. It happened just a bit sooner this time.

What happened to me was that the realisation of not being able to control the destiny of who was dearest to me had a momentary and shocking impact on my entire being. I was suddenly confronted with something bigger than me.

While my reaction was indeed to worrying circumstances of human health, it can just as well be viewed as a metaphor for any situation in which we prefer control over trust in the outcomes of things that matter and with the people who are in any way involved in them. Despite knowing that it is all absolutely beyond our control.

In the few months after the diagnosis, we visited more doctors than we had done since Noa was born. That required a lot of resilience from our entire family. It required us to accept that what really makes life worth living is to know and honour what we passionately believe in, rather than a frenetic drive to control our outcomes, which more often than not represent uncontrollable circumstances. One such uncontrollable circumstance is in fact life itself, that is too uncontrollable for actual safety to be anything other than an inner feeling. Even when the stakes are at their highest.

Life eventually requires unconditional trust in something bigger than us. While we are deceiving ourselves that we are in control of so many daily details, one piece of news – just one single piece of news – is sufficient to disarm the illusion of control that we may have based our entire livelihood on. When that happens, a belief that life is lived in two ways – either by controlling or by creating and that while the latter is risky, the former is not life at all – may be the only substantial thing we have to hold on to as we move through the discomfort of living and leading.

And if there's anywhere leaders are required, it's in discomfort. In his book *Tribes*, Seth Godin says when you identify the discomfort, you've found the place where a leader is needed.[54] Because true leaders, bold ones, have the capacity to allow for whatever there is in the discomfort – to just be. They allow circumstances, emotions, reactions to simply exist and they have the capacity to stay with them. This is the capacity to "stay with" that is eventually required to transform ourselves and our worlds. It's the power required to allow growth.

It's about staying with the circumstances that go beyond and longer than a single moment. And it's about not controlling them. Simply *be with* them for as long as they last to allow what may to happen, beyond our control. Staying in that space that looks, feels, sounds, smells and tastes uncontrollable as we as leaders ask: What do I choose to trust? And then also: What do we choose to trust together?

I understand that this concept may be confronting for some leaders who are very much self-sufficient and tend to perceive responsibility and control as terms with equal meaning. I urge you to differentiate between acting responsibly with trust in an overall positive outcome versus losing your presence and your focus by being attached to the outcome that you cannot actually control. That is how we allow things to happen from the place of trust rather than suffer from the place of impossible control.

While our family was waiting for the surgery of our son and taking all the necessary actions in a highly responsible manner, we were also staying with all the discomfort of the situation, allowing for life to beautifully happen on many other different levels. We chose to trust what we could not control and we chose to do so together.

People were sometimes surprised at the calmness of our reaction as we were approaching the surgery date. I dare to think they even went as far as to doubt we cared because we were not trying to madly control it. Oh, we did care. We cared beyond words. Believe me. It was just the power of "staying with" that we relied on and really just – trusted. That's how we chose to lead ourselves and each other in this situation larger than life.

Controlling happens in the absence of trust. It accompanies the inability to let go of our idea of what the outcome must be for us. The perfect one, the right one, the one apparently controlled by us. That's our inability to detach ourselves from what we have designed as the result. I've seen so many leaders wasting the power of their amazing will by imprisoning it in their relentless need to control what they know is uncontrollable. They know, but they refuse to accept it. As I learnt from my mentor: they're not stuck. They are just stubborn.

Even when we are absolutely aware that it does not depend upon the one who's leading, the ones who are being led or anyone around us, it is still so hard to accept that there's nothing we can do about the destiny of those things or people that matter so much. And what makes it so hard is us, who forget that we can trust.

Our trust is allowing life, work, miracles if you wish, to simply happen. We chose to trust in a good future that was going to be created outside our control. What was hidden in this choice was our readiness to let go of whatever past experience or way of operating there was that might have been affecting our trust in a good future perspective.

Imagine, if you would, just approaching your team in this way today. Your family. Your community. Any aspect of your world. Imagine if you could stop trying to control your relationships, and understand them instead as the playground for your collective leadership that requires you to trust in whatever is emerging out of their dynamics.

In my own story, I could so easily have slipped into my desire to control my behaviour, my son's behaviour, my spouse's behaviour, my son's grandparents' behaviour... I could so easily have slipped into the intention to figure out and then sort out everything about this situation that had potentially many unsortable elements.

Or I could have allowed for our relationship to happen: for us to grow through it, to notice what the learning was for all of us, collectively. How it would make us stronger or weaker or something else. Accepting the complexity of this situation and the way it added complexity to our relationships, I could hold the sense of direction and remain open to allow any change to happen to my idea of how it should eventually be. And I could trust in what was bigger than all of us involved. It wasn't easy. But do you know any other way? And still, it was as hard as it was eventually liberating, depending on how you approach it.

I see, on a daily basis, leaders that are trying really hard to control the relationships within their teams. Sometimes, when they are ready to step back from their own desire to save the team, when they are ready to simply let go, they allow for things to fall into their place. That also is an important leadership capacity that speaks for their ability to trust as opposed to their attachment to the hero leader self-image.

Our trust in whatever is larger than us is the ultimate act of getting out of our own way and allowing our leadership to happen. A very capable client of mine was struggling to trust in the outcome of what was very important for her. She had to stand up in front of the leadership team and speak about what matters to her. When she finally did it, this is how she explained her experience: "It felt as if I was out of my body. There was me speaking and I was looking at what she was doing, seeing her going forward, not stopping. I was out of my own body."

That is the best definition that I've heard so far of how to get out of your own way and trust that exactly that will allow your leadership to actually happen. Letting go of your already ex-self, to allow your next level self to come to the surface. Let go to let come.

"Let go to let come" is a concept from Otto Scharmer's *Theory U: Leading from the Future as It Emerges*, in which he talks about the open will as an instrument our society needs in order to become "a part of the story of the future rather than holding on to and embodying the story of the past".[55] The open will is the capacity to let go of old ways of doing things and accept new ones.

The "let go to let come" concept requires from leaders an openness to trust in what is bigger than us, our present and our past and what wants to emerge from our future. That stands for allowing the future to happen through trust in something that differs from our firm, fixed, and known intentions and something that's beyond the control of our doing or our mere rational figuring out.

It is enough to think of the true uncontrollable nature of life for us to become aware, in an instant, of the limitations and sufferings we encounter in our living and leading when we deprive ourselves of this dimension of trust.

Empowering nature of trust

There is something enormously empowering about trust. And so, when we choose to disregard any of the three layers of trust, what we deprive ourselves of is the many successes that could have otherwise happened on the wings of empowerment.

A great deal of what impacts our success is the sense of empowerment. And by trusting we empower the three elements for success: ourselves, others and whatever is bigger than us – our relationship, our project, our vision. When leaders refuse to choose this for a number of rational reasons that they provide themselves with, it's often because what they prioritise is to be right rather than being in the service of whatever needs to be achieved, made or created.

We have all experienced doubts in the outcome of many events and collaborations. It's normal; it's human. And what's radical is to consciously exchange that doubt with trust, thus being trustful about our own decisions and actions, believing in another to help us become just as bold and creative as we trust – even before we see – them to genuinely be, and setting up whatever we're doing together for success. That's how everyone and everything gets empowered. Empowerment leads to magic, or the magic of success if you wish. And magic begins with many layers of trust engaged by us as leaders, by choice.

Trust is a choice. Leadership is a decision.

Trust is a choice. Leadership is a decision. And then life comes as a reward together with freedom and the liberating sense of courage.

We came to understand this as we sent our six-year-old warrior son for heart surgery. A super-energetic little boy who never had any symptoms, who always looked fine, but in essence, he was not so. That appearance made it even harder to decide. We could have left room for millions of doubts. Instead, we chose trust. Trust is a choice. In situations like this one, that becomes crystal clear.

As leaders we make decisions that impact other people's lives. As much as this one came from our parental responsibility, it still was a decision made for somebody else's life. His, not ours. Perhaps our son could have lived into his thirties perfectly fine. Perhaps not. No one knows the price he would have to pay for our comfort zone in which we avoided taking a decision. Just as no one was able to predict the final outcome of our courage. That's how the leadership game works.

It was the hardest decision we have ever had to make in our family and we made that decision with our full commitment to the situation, choosing to trust that it was the right one.

Choosing to trust in the person who was going to stop his heart for fifty minutes during a six-hour-long surgery. Choosing to trust that this person would trust himself to patch it up perfectly and bring it back to life. Choosing to trust that something bigger than us and that person had our son's back that day.

I'll never forget waving at him outside the operating theatre, as I guess no parent ever does in such circumstances.

And there we were, left in a state of expectancy, detached from expectations. Such a paradox, especially when the stakes are so high. The only ally one has in such a paradoxical state is, again, trust.

Choosing trust was a hard choice and the reality is that beyond the physical point where you are allowed to accompany your child before he enters the operating room, you cannot control any of the expectations. It is the point at which the illusionary nature of control comes as a pretty real slap in the face.

When choosing trust, what you receive instead of that slap is the opportunity to be intentional, conscious and boldly alive to be able to create your next Self and your next circumstances.

We made the decision for our son. And then we had to retake it every second in our heads, our hearts and our guts. As we moved forward with our full commitment, we had to keep surrendering to the trust we had chosen. Recovering quickly every time we slipped. Because that's how the leadership game works.

In our own time and at our own pace, each one of us – my husband, our son, myself and all others involved – was welcoming our own next level Self that we had decided to create in the given circumstances.

Our choice to trust eventually rewarded us with life.

Your reflection

Here are a few questions to reflect on:

1. What is trusting yourself? What is it to trust those you lead? What is it to trust the outcome?

2. What is it to trust unconditionally? What is your alternative to unconditional trust?

3. What needs to change in you, to understand trust as choice?

4. What else requires you to pause and reflect?

CHAPTER 6: Calling Forth

LEADERSHIP IN RADICAL connection makes calling others forth one of the greatest possible acts of love and care. Leadership is an invitation for loving confrontation. If any part of that term is lacking in the way you lead, you need to challenge yourself on how much you see, hear, love and trust others.

You cannot call someone forth unless you hold a bigger vision for their life and work and you invite their brilliant potential, in which you undoubtedly believe. You believe in those people's wholeness and resourcefulness in a matter-of-fact way, and you call them forth to make their actions show up equally as whole and resourceful as they are themselves. More than anything else, calling forth is thus a mindset. And it is the one so much needed in our world.

The definition of calling forth could therefore be: call someone to come forward in their magnificence.

In the context of leadership, this definition sounds like an inevitable element in the development of people. And yet, much more than seeing them calling their people forth, we see leaders calling them *out*.

Instead of taking a stand for their people's potential, leaders often assume an attitude of judgement and criticism towards those they lead. They seem to have a well-developed muscle for calling others out and an underdeveloped consciousness for calling them forth.

And we all go through situations in which we demonstrate a potential gap between who we truly are and what we currently bring. Calling forth requires leaders to be very present with their people, so that they can notice this gap and ideally approach those they lead with this message: "YOU are whole. YOUR actions in this case are broken. There's a gap in between who you are and how you act. This creates an unintended impact when in fact what we need more of or less of from you is this! How will you show up to close the gap? And what support do you need?" That's really about loving people and calling them forth to their development.

Leaders always close gaps, starting with their own, in between what leadership is and what it is not. It's called growth. By calling others forth, they help them do the same.

Hard-loving truth

Calling someone forth requires giving them hard-loving truth and that's what makes calling forth a challenge. However, hard-loving truth is not a harsh approach, but rather a sign of deep connection. It's important to understand that a hard-loving truth stands for a conversation grounded in integrity and intimacy.

Leaders offer their people a hard-loving truth because they undoubtedly believe in their potential and wish to see them grow to its level. More than wishing, they are determined to wholeheartedly support them in that growth and that is why they are sharing the hard-loving truth with them. Your willingness and ability to share hard-loving truth is an essential part of your leadership, and it speaks largely about your integrity as a leader, your inclusive mindset and your ability to connect at the risk of vulnerability and exposure.

Hard-loving truth lives in radical openness and because radical openness is needed but not always comfortable, hard-loving truth often comes together with discomfort. That makes it part of what you may call tough conversations.

In many corporate cultures tough conversations are avoided because people do not feel safe enough in their workplace to be able to have them. This is where the paradox occurs: the less tough conversations there are, the less safety there is in the workplace. That is exactly how what's not being shared and talked about designs your leadership much more than the discomfort of what is. And so, hard-loving truth in all its discomfort is in fact a way of increasing safety among those leading and being led. Readiness to bring the hard-loving truth despite discomfort assures everyone that no topic will be avoided and this automatically creates safety.

Hard-loving truth is also what every leader will tell you they get too little of at the top. If you are one of those leaders claiming you do not get enough hard-loving truth, this is what I'm curious about: How much of that hard-loving truth are you sharing with others? And how about with yourself? At the risk of sounding like a cliché, leaders do lead by example. So, ask yourself in this context, what in fact are you modelling with your relationship to fierce love when it comes to sharing feedback or opening up tough conversations? Sharing hard-loving truth requires openness to vulnerability on the side of both the giver and the receiver. Often it pushes both parties into the depths that they fear to go to. Being equipped with integrity, compassion and gratitude is what turns these depths, these dark places, into a gold mine of everyone's development as opposed to a bottomless pit.

Listening to lots of leaders' stories in my work, I've realised that in the absence of hard-loving truth it is most likely silence or criticism that the leaders choose to share. And for me that always poses a question of caring. Leaders share hard-loving truth when they truly care about those they lead. Daring to know something about other people's unintended impact is bold. Sharing it is exposing. As much as it does not seem so, it can be more exposing for the one who offers than for the one who receives.

So, in order to take the risk of telling hard-loving truth to others, as with any risk, something more important has to prevail. My experience taught me that it is deep care about and connection with the other that has us face the risk and discomfort of the hard-loving truth. If we're not bringing it, it's not because we cannot say it, as much as it is because we do not care enough about the one who needs to hear it.

My longing for you

We know that we care about the other when we hold a longing for them.

A room of thousands of dreams

Every single heart in that room was beating fast and our faces were radiant. The space was filled with love. More than love, it was filled with undoubted dreams. Have you ever experienced a room of thousands of dreams about the bright future in which every single person holds nothing but an undisputed belief in their achievement?

Around twenty of us were standing in a circle facing each other. It felt as if we were swimming in each other's eyes. A deep look and even a deeper breath and you could hear the room murmuring: let me share my longing for you...

In that very moment you could see the other person, the one on the receiving end, crying blissful tears about the promising future of a bigger self. Only because the one offering it made the future sound not only promising but entirely certain. It sounded so clear and so possible from another person's mouth, from another person's heart. Hearing what they so bravely and undoubtedly held as your future achievement.

That was my first coaching training that taught me about the power of longing for other people and what can be created when you dare to share it, what it means for the individual and what its collective impact is. Later on, I went through a similar experience on another course and there was one thing that the process always included: looking the other person in the eyes. Seeing their soul and knowing its desires even without any words involved. From a pure human connection, you were able to offer them a future story of their fulfilled potential, thus inviting their greatness in the moment.

So, how is it possible to know and share that?

Leaders always dare to know and their knowing in this case comes from their caring. Leaders have genuine interest in people, in their stories hidden behind their words and their current deeds. They are interested to the point that they have a longing that is important to share.

Stop, think and feel for a moment. In your mind, see the faces of the people you lead. Meet their eyes. What is it that you are longing for them? Have you ever shared it with them and if you haven't what would make it worth doing so? What would be their magnificence that you would in that way invite to come forward? Much of the coaching process is inviting people's raw, human, bold magnificence to come to the surface. Even when their shadow side is revealed to them through a hard-loving truth, it is only really done to invite their light.

At this point, many leaders will refer to the lack of time to dedicate to such leadership. Overpacked business realities can be a wonderful excuse to drive our awareness away from the fact that we ourselves always dictate to a greater extent what they will be overpacked with. When it comes to caring connection, time is an excuse, a protecting shield that helps us remain at a safe distance for reasons very different from the lack of time. When leaders' hearts are sensitive to their people's stories, their clocks adjust.

Longing is therefore very much about listening. There is one thing about listening that keeps astonishing me and that is what almost seems to be an obsession of the corporate world with what they call *active* listening. They often express the wish to learn skills for better active listening. I have not managed to understand how listening can be anything but active because at a minimum, listening is an action, something that you do, and is therefore active.

The real question is *who* you are actively listening to in the process: yourself, the other or even the story behind what others are bringing. And that's when listening really becomes a presence with another person. This presence is the highest level of what could be called active listening. You are listening to the other person to the point that you are hearing your longing for them. And once you embrace yourself in the role of having longing for other people and daring to express it, even a deep look into a stranger's eyes will suffice to access that knowing.

Knowing and expressing the longing for the other person changes the one who offers it as much as the one who receives it. If hard-loving truth is the path from integrity to intimacy, then having and communicating longing is the act of deepening the intimacy. Another level of making your leadership relational, making it real, vulnerable and powerfully spacious for everyone to grow.

Seeing, hearing and feeling the bigger and bolder other, and calling their bigger and bolder identity forth is an act of deep human care. Leaders, what is your longing for those you lead?

What I long for you

We were completing our eight-month-long developmental coaching programme that day. The person I got to know as a highly driven perfectionist leader at the end of the previous year was now sitting in silence opposite me. Just in that moment I was thinking how it had been quite a ride when he spoke: "This has been a bumpy ride. An eye-opening one I won't forget."

"So, what's the knowing now?" I asked.

"I feel I know what matters to me. And I'm finally able to accept it. To accept me. And also understand them," he said, referring to people in his workplace, at which point his chin shook and his eyes filled with tears. He was in deep connection with himself, with his very core and everything that lived there. Everything that mattered. He had arrived home to himself and, much more important than me being able to fully see and hear him, he was able to experience himself.

When we had our first conversation a few months before that, his attitude of righteousness was palpable in the room as it was his rejection of the coaching work. There was a bit of curiosity in him; still, at times I felt as if it was only his curiosity about what else in his own development he could fight against. What else he could resist.

That day, eight months later, there was a leader facing me in his inner authority that was strong and human. As if the connection button had been switched on by himself because he was assured that getting in touch with his own heart would not melt him but rather ground him in – as he kept repeating – what truly mattered to him.

"Your energy is powerful beyond words," I began and it had an impact on him right out of the gate. "To suffocate that energy under the excuse of being too much would not serve either you or your company or your entire world. We would lose you and more importantly you would lose yourself. And that would be the closest to failure that we could all get."

He was breathing in my words as I continued: "And sometimes when that essence of you takes the shape of a tremendous drive, it can start breaking rather than building." He nodded as a sign that he was hearing familiar news.

"And so, my longing for you is that you learn how to tap into your true essential passion in the middle of your drive, as if you'd laser-focus on the very core of what truly matters to you. What I want for you is, that you let that part of you be the key aspect that you'll bring out to others. And I dare to know that when you demonstrate such leadership you will engage every single person in your presence as they – instead of running away from your drive – get inspired by your passion."

He straightened his back and went through the discomfort of looking me straight in the eyes. In that moment, a bigger and bolder version of himself confidently smiled.

Leaning into each other

Imagine a triangle as the most stable structure. In fact, imagine an equilateral one as the most stable of all triangles. Notice the two vertical sides pressed against each other and just for a moment in your mind replace them with two real people. As you've done that you see them now pressing their fingertips against each other. Perhaps you see their feet fidgeting a bit as they attempt to find the right place and their bodies take the right inclination angle. It can seem messy for a while.

And then as they find their position, you realise that what you're looking at is each of them holding all of the other person while offering all of themselves in return. At the very same time. You can see two people leaning into each other and using their bodies to represent trust as they call each other forth in the moment.

Now imagine the actual level of trust between them as they stand in that position. A tiny little step going a bit too far forward or backwards, and they could both fall flat on their face. Finding the right balance in holding the other and offering oneself is crucial. It seems like a sophisticated skill of being fully attentive to the other and to oneself at the same time.

And then, they connect through their trust. No one is withholding and no one is over-pushing. It's not a game of having power over the other or giving it away. They have power *with* each other and, just like an equilateral triangle, they are stable. Standing in that position, their eyes can easily meet and they can tell how invested the other one is by how far they are leaning in or holding back. They clearly feel the level of their engagement.

They can notice how much they both care about what they are co-creating. It's a moment of exposure and vulnerability. They know this as they hear questions within themselves: Can I trust you? Will you hold me? Will I be able to hold you? They also know they can ask for help at any moment in service of their collective stability. Asking for help will be welcomed and embraced, not judged.

By leaning into their relationship, they confirm they know what it is that they can count on from each other. Being able to share the hard-loving truth and know their longings for each other is what will restore their faith if for a moment they happen to lose balance. And before you know it, they are present again to each other and to their relationship. Their stability is again being co-created in the moment by them fully leaning into one another.

Doesn't this remind you of leadership happening in radical connection?

The steps can sometimes be clumsy and messy but the essence is about bringing your full self and accepting all of the other in your relationship. When you lean into each other you are invested in standing in your own brilliance and invitingly holding the magnificence of the other. If there is an absence of readiness to make such an investment, leaning into cannot take place. Because there is no relationship to create from. There is no connection that you both have a stake in.

Leaning into each other may well be the deepest expression of trust and intimacy in leadership. There are no easy shortcuts to it. It is as risky as it sounds. Taking the path that eventually leads into the power of trust, transparency and meaningful co-creation, everyone who is involved first needs to go through the discomfort of letting go of control and asking for help, to name just two. That is what makes leadership: rather than a waste of energy on protecting oneself, an investment into growing everyone.

The leadership described in the realm of ***Other*** is also what makes it an investment into growing world peace. And if you have, for an instant, judged this statement as an exaggeration, perhaps it's time to remind you of Mahatma Ghandi's quote: "With every true friendship, we build more firmly the foundations on which the peace of the whole world rests."

We do indeed. By leading each other in radical connection, we build a peaceful home we all want to live in. We shape its foundations together. By seeing each other, trusting each other and inviting each other's great human potential, by experiencing each other, we can better see, hear and feel any underlying concern about what needs to be built or rebuilt, shaped or reshaped in any aspect of our world. It is how we sense the invitation for creating our individual and collective contribution.

And it is again in our connection that we find the ultimate inspiration and the purpose to actually create it.

Your reflection

Here are a few questions to reflect on:

1. What's waiting to be called forth in you?
2. What is it that you're longing for the people you lead and live with?
3. What does it mean to truly lean into others?
4. What else requires you to pause and reflect?

Before proceeding to Part 3, here's an invitation for you:

Great leaders are great coaches.

Visit www.boldleadership-culture.com and schedule a strategy call with me to discuss how to bring the **Coaching Consciousness Training Programme** to your organisation and teach your leaders the coaching mindset and the coaching language.

PART 3 UNIVERSE

Leadership is not a matter of power.
It's a matter of concern.

A home we don't want to live in

Many leaders that I work with, and particularly those on lower levels, pause when faced with the question: "Help me understand, how is it that you're shaping your organisation?" That is when we open up the conversation about power and concern.

If you stay with the concepts of power and concern for a moment, you're very likely to realise that there is an underlying belief in many of us that carries much of this message: in order to demonstrate the concern, one has to have power.

This is a very non-accountable, victim-like perspective.

If you are a leader in the full capacity of your soul, of your amazing potential, then we will see you holding a very different belief in the realm of ***Universe***. Rather than waiting for the formal authority to grant you permission to actively and continuously attempt to make changes about what concerns you in your environment, you will do it based on your leadership accountability. You are a leader who cares about the common greater good and you take personal risks for it. A lot of what this personal risk consists of is questioning many things and courageously bringing the topics to the table to speak about that which others do not dare to. Simply because what's happening in the universe, as a metaphor for your context, concerns you and you – as a part of it – feel accountable to act.

It is your choice as a leader to attach dimensionality to the term universe. You can look at it as if you were looking at some concrete particles or a wider less defined space. In other words, it may refer to your family, your team, your organisation, your community, your country, the entire globe, or the entire undivided space of everything that is material and non-material. It is not about the dimension; it is about your accountability to act in whatever universe dimension is your focus. The dimension is your leadership choice; the accountability is the essence of your leadership. And, as often happens, leaders who feel truly courageously accountable for any dimension of their universe pretty much feel concern for every dimension of it.

Being a leader in the realm of ***Universe*** means knowing that our world is actually being shaped and impacted by how much we act on something that is of interest and importance. And that happens even when we do not possess some sort of status, a certain formal authority that we automatically associate with the ability to make change.

In fact, there are many examples of brave people who have dared to speak up about important crises in the face of the entire world, challenging the authorities and inspiring everyone who pauses to listen to their stories.

This also relates to the importance of sharing our stories in the process of shaping the world as our home. It is through the human stories that we've often witnessed the power of concern winning over the power of status. Sometimes, these are very serious stories indicating strong concern over high-impact issues. Whatever the stories are, I choose to trust that each time we do see someone speaking truth to power out of their concern, we get inspired to raise our own voice too to better our corner of the world. One story at the time, no matter how big or small.

Here are a few of such inspiring, bold stories.

Amariyanna Copeny, born in 2007, raised awareness about Flint's ongoing water crisis. The water was not properly treated and was therefore causing water supply contamination because of the lead leaking. At the age of eight, Little Miss Flint, which is what she was known as, wrote a letter to US President Barack Obama that resulted in him eventually authorising $100 million to help fix the crisis. Obama responded to her with the words "kids like you are what makes me optimistic about the future".[56]

Ethiopian writer Befeqadu Hailu wrote about many cases of brutality and human rights violations by the Ethiopian state. Hailu won the 2012 Burt Award for African Literature with his novel *Children of Their Parents.* He was also imprisoned and charged first with "terrorism" for his writing and then with "inciting violence through writing". Hailu continued to write. In 2019 he was named International Writer of Courage at the PEN Pinter Prize ceremony where he said: "No war, no campaign has more power than writing to change the world without claiming lives."[57]

In 2019 six activists, each with their own cause, united together for the youth summit at the United Nations in Geneva. One of them was Memory Banda, fighting forced child marriage after watching her younger sister get married at the age of eleven. Banda helped to change the law in Malawi, leaving us with this important message: "If we do nothing now, then there is nothing for the future."[58]

And yet, many times – even though exposed to many bold human stories – we choose nothing for the future and succumb to our apparent powerlessness because of what it momentarily represents: less risk.

It starts from the protective stories we tell ourselves. Regardless of how these stories may differ for each one of us, one of the lines seems to be the same: it does not concern me. In other words, it does not affect me. It does not directly affect the world I live in either.

And so, there's a list of examples that go from the apparently distant reality to one that is closer to us. The continuous poverty of another continent does not concern me. Racial injustice going on in the other corner of the world does not concern me. War and genocide happening in neighbouring countries do not concern me. Home violence in the local community does not concern me. Abuse of any kind in the organisation, perhaps in the office right next to mine, does not concern me. I'm sure you can continue the list. We all can. The truth is, it always concerns everyone and it always affects everyone. Because it is shaping the world that is the home to any one of us. This home being our planet, our countries, our neighbourhoods, our organisations, our teams, our own families.

But because we believe that it is not about our wholeness and it does not concern us personally, we remain silent in the presence of whatever we see happening. And we need justification for this silence. Once again, we need a story, but this time to help us make the silence our only legitimate choice. So, to be able to live with our own chosen silence in front of what we see and don't consider right, we build our story from "It does not concern me" to "I can't do anything about it. I've got no power and I won't make any difference anyhow." And here another line of our story gets instantly created and it says: my voice does not matter. Therefore, I won't even try to use it to give voice to the unspoken.

We so willingly embrace this illusion of powerlessness. We even seem not to question this distortive truth, according to which acting on what's compromising the universal values in our world is almost considered as an act of unreasonableness. Instead of choosing to be consciously bold, we choose the path of protecting ourselves from being what we label as unreasonable. What a successful way to give our power away.

As by choice we're diving into powerlessness disguised as reason, there seems to be one final punch line we need in this journey away from humanity. It starts with the question: "And why would I? Why would I risk?"

Indeed, why would you? Why would any of us risk what feels safe and comfortable for something that we have convinced ourselves does not concern us in the first place and we have no power to change? This is how we choose conformity over integrity based on the final line of our story: conformity is reasonable.

From that moment on our silence becomes our most powerful weapon in creating the disconnection from ourselves and others. By deepening the unspoken, we initiate the work on destroying the universal values we collectively crave for. We start making our contribution to shaping the universe that looks like a home we don't actually want to live in.

It all started with: it doesn't concern me. And there's another way to live and lead in this world and its systems. The way that is bolder.

CHAPTER 7:
The Concern

BOLD LEADERS' STORY about concern is different. Bold leaders are focused on the entire system they live and work in, knowing that whatever they do or don't do represents their contribution to what the system will eventually look like. Instead of the system, you can use any other word to bring this concept closer to your reality, such as your organisation, your team, your community, or any other aspect of your world.

Whatever it is, if you are a bold leader, your world can count on you for at least two promises.

Firstly, that you are awake. Secondly, that you are committed to service.

Two promises

Your first promise as a bold leader is that you are fully present with your world's needs. You are a curious and watchful observer of whatever is going on in your environment and beyond. That could be a single issue in your closest community or it could be something much larger on a global scale. It's not about the dimension of it; it's about how much it gets into your focus because it holds something that matters to you. You feel it concerns you because it concerns your world. You direct your attention to it to sense what is going on, what wants to happen, and what your role is in it. The gap in between that existing and emerging reality is what cannot go unnoticed for you. Closing that gap calls for your bold leadership.

Your second promise shows what you firmly believe leadership as such is. As a bold leader you believe in leadership as one of the highest forms of service to others, and therefore service to your world. You are decisively committed to engage your leadership to primarily serve that world whose needs you are aware of.

Let's for a moment look at the concept of leadership as a service from two perspectives. The term "servant leadership" was created by Robert K. Greenleaf: "The servant-leader is servant first... It begins with the natural feeling that one wants to serve, to serve first. Then conscious choice brings one to aspire to lead."[59] Greenleaf continues to speak about a difference between the leader who is a leader-first and the one who is a servant-first and says: "The difference manifests itself in the care taken by the servant-first to make sure that other people's highest priority needs are being served."[60]

Another perspective on leaders serving the world is in my view the one that speaks about the meeting point of leaders' needs and the world's needs. In his book *Play Your Bigger Game*, Rick Tamlyn writes about recognising where the leader's hunger for something intersects with the hunger in some parts of their world.[61] In other words, it's something that you're hungry for and you realise that the world is too. Acting on what both you and your world need means serving your world with your very purpose through your leadership.

I believe that bold leaders' service is a journey that goes from deep caring to courageous creating. As the ones committed to serve with their leadership, they start their work from caring about what they sense is needed in their environment. And they dare to know what that is, because it matters to them too. They are awake to what is existing and emerging within and around them and they are ready to act on it, and create from it. Often this journey starts with their conscious choice to speak up despite the risk.

Hearing all these perspectives, notice the gap between the belief of not being concerned about what's going on and the one of being committed to serve with one's leadership in whatever is going on in the world. That is the gap that bold leaders close. It's the gap that represents a journey from indifference to caring and eventually serving.

Just like caring and serving, indifference is also a choice. We choose to believe that many things happening in our world that we, deep down, don't approve of, do not really affect us and that our response to them, based on such a belief, equally has no contribution to creating exactly that world in which things we don't approve of continue to happen. Such a choice makes our indifference to a number of pains and injustices around us, well, easier to swallow.

Bold leaders shake up the comfort of indifference for the sake of change: for the sake of a different contribution and the creation of a different environment. That's how they care and that's how they serve. No matter the risk. In fact, the very reason why we need bold leaders is because of their readiness to risk their safety for the sake of their service to their world, be it as small as their department, or as big as the planet. And so, it's not the size of the issue that counts but rather the leaders' promises that make others count on them: their awareness of what's needed and their commitment to serve it.

When assessing the effectiveness of individual leaders, there is a competency that refers to the presence of these promises in their leadership. We find it in the Leadership Circle Profile™[62] dimension called Systems Awareness[63] and it measures the degree to which leaders' awareness is focused on improving the entire system and on community welfare. One leadership competency within this dimension is called Community Concern.[64] It is one of the key competencies needed in the leadership of today's world.

Community Concern measures leaders' orientation to serve their world with their leadership. Even without knowing their leadership assessment results, we would most probably recognise those leaders who score highly on this competency by their enormous positive influence and their ability to inspire. Their caring would be evident regardless of whether there's a minor issue at play or something as wide and as deep as saving the world. I believe that leaders who score highly on Community Concern consciously bring to life their two promises: being awake and serving.

Living these promises is an intentional leadership journey. One that starts with a choice to believe that something, even though it may not be affecting me on the most direct level, still affects me because it affects someone in the world that we all share together.

The charm of conformity

Honouring our concern starts with embracing the idea that we can actually do something about whatever we wish to see changed in the world around us. We embrace that idea with our two intentions – being awake and of service – thus keeping our two promises to the world as bold leaders. In addition to being awake to what's going on in our world and committed to be in service, there is a part of us that holds answers to the question: What is it that really concerns me about this? The part that knows the answer is our integrity.

Integrity creates a powerful impact in leadership and it's the impact of trust. Can we count on you to bring the truth from the heart to both yourself and us? And can we rely on you to speak up and act from that place no matter the risk? Can we be sure that you won't be selective with the truth depending on who's listening? Then, we can trust you as a leader. Then, we can feel you're acting out of your integrity instead of compromising it for the sake of safe conformity.

However, the reality has shown us that the charm of conformity is an ever-present human temptation. Looking at the source of this choice from a neuroscience perspective, we understand it stands for our human need to belong. We can further measure the tendency to belong through Leadership Circle Profile™[65], thus measuring our need to obey the rules, and meet the expectations of whoever we see as an external authority. In order to feel that we belong to a group of people, be it an organisation, our team, our community or our family, we need to live by the standards, rules and values of that group – we need to conform. And that, often, means boxing in our own bold leadership to what seems a collectively good idea. That also means giving up on our two bold promises of being awake and in service by exchanging them for another promise – the one of fitting in.

Speaking about good ideas, Chris Argyris, an American business theorist known for his seminal work on learning organisations, said that "the most fundamental assumption of the underground managerial world is that truth is a good idea when it is not embarrassing or threatening – the very conditions under which truth is especially needed". He continues by saying that many management organisations "create, by their own choice, a world that is contrary to what they say they prefer... as if they are compulsively tied to a set of processes that prevent them from changing what they believe they should change".[66]

This is the conversation about us collectively creating a home we don't actually wish to live in. We seem to conform to what's publicly assumed to have to be for whatever reasonable explanation we've given ourselves, instead of boldly speaking up about what's intimately known, felt and believed to be truly collectively needed.

The truth is that small acts of anything, be it safe conformity or bold integrity, shape the world over time. All those small acts represent our choice and bold leaders are awake to their own choice by seeking a deeper meaning behind it: What service am I doing to my world by my acts of conformity and my acts of integrity? Bold leaders choose consciously and courageously. They choose to act with conviction.

And so, the answer to this question helps them resolve a tension: the one between the integrity that feels right and brings aliveness and potential risk, and the conformity that often feels blandly reasonable.

Unreasonableness

Unreasonable or consciously bold?

"Here's the thing. You know what I want to see more of from you?" he shouted straightforwardly, with the answer waiting to burst out of him in what I assumed would be an even louder voice. I heard that loudness pushing against the walls of the training room and for a moment I was unsure if that was the echo of his voice or my own heart pulsating at the discomfort of what I might hear next.

I didn't answer anything because I knew it wasn't really a question that he expected an answer to. He was my front of the room leader in the leadership development retreat where vulnerability was served three times a day, at a minimum. I trusted him deeply. I knew that the impact of edginess he had would always be coupled with the important truth.

"Un-rea-son-able-ness." I guess he said it in such a way as to imprint those syllables on my mind and my heart, and then he continued: "You are so reasonable. Everything that you do is so reasonable. Like a super good work of art that has never allowed itself to be a masterpiece."

He paused. So did I and so did the rest of the room.

"Go crazy for once, go big, go bold! Go and do unreasonable stuff that your soul is craving for! Your world needs what you're craving for." I guess that by then he was already shouting. I'm not really sure because that was the point from which I switched to listening to the other voice, the one inside me. It said: "Whatever you do, just be clever. Be clever." A life-long mantra instilled into me from my very early childhood. Be clever. Whatever you do. Oh, in a split second it made sense. I connected the dots.

And as I did, my inner conversation went on: "But what does it mean to be clever? Not to rock the boat? Not to go against? Never to confront? But I've been born to question and confront. We all have. So, now, what do I do with that part of me? Do I switch it off as if it doesn't exist? Do I just shut down that desire in me that's the source of all meaning and aliveness? Do I make sure I don't lose my best life yet by never daring to create it and serve the world with it? Ok, I've got it: I'm calling it being reasonable." I lifted my head just to see those smiling faces around me. It felt as if they were offering me permission to start being unreasonable. It was easy to accept their offer because I'd just granted it to myself within.

They say we've got two lives. The other one begins once we realise it's only ONE life that we really have. From that moment on in my life, I confronted myself with this question every time I had to make an important choice: Am I being unreasonable or am I being consciously bold?

I trust I have many more years to face this dilemma and live to see the outcome in many different contexts. So far, this compass has not let me down.

This is how George Bernard Shaw put it: "The reasonable man adapts himself to the world. The unreasonable one persists in trying to adapt the world to himself. Therefore, all progress depends on the unreasonable man." In line with these words, we can recognise that unreasonable man in a bold leader.

Bold leaders have a different relationship with unreasonableness. In their mindset, unreasonableness stands for a hint, an alarm signal to question. And so, they ask: What potentially wants to emerge that this team, or organisation, or whatever group of people is showing resistance to? It's their curiosity and their boldness taking the lead here. Their willingness to embrace this question takes them from a safe conformity to what may become an uncomfortable but very much needed confrontation.

Just as with unreasonableness, bold leaders have a different relationship with confrontation as well. They hold a belief that confrontation is a path to creativity and meaningful work through radically open conversations, which is exactly what we need more of in all of our communities, in all of our systems. What we have instead of radically open conversations most of the time is artificially harmonious discussions, which are an outstanding tool to collectively create what we collectively don't want.

They are a perfect space to discourage anyone from daring to truly lead and encourage everyone to rather choose disengaged followship. Sometimes it's even called alignment and celebrated as such with full disregard for its frequent devastating outcome: instead of talking to one another, people start talking about each other. Instead of connecting to each other, they connect to the anger, disappointment and emptiness within.

Contrary to that, the path to true and meaningful alignment often goes through confrontation, through bolder, better and more creative solutions that are being shaped as we confront ourselves and each other. So that we can talk to each other and hear each other, allowing us to eventually meaningfully align around what we sense is collectively needed.

That is why bold leaders dare to have a good reason to be unreasonable rebels in many systems that too often want everyone to fall for the charms of conformity. Their reason is their concern about the collective world and their service to its best version yet.

In acting out of this service, bold leaders pave the road from reasonable conformity to potentially risky integrity with a purpose. Their purpose is brought to life by a great step away from self-interest and safety-craving ego towards radical humanity and risky openness for the collective benefit.

Truly bold leaders invite confrontation instead of conformity for the sake of truth because they want to hear and say the truth for the sake of change. And they want to see the change for the sake of growth and experience growth to find meaning. Their mission, in the broadest sense, is to inspire meaning on the collective level. Their vision is always a more meaningful world.

Seeing them through this lens, we would be right to name them servant rebels and describe them as consciously bold souls acting from a place of integrity to be the warriors of a meaningful and sustainable home we willingly share together. I've chosen to find the ultimate definition of such warrior leaders in the words of Martin Luther King, Jr. who, describing the moment in which an individual starts living, said it does not happen "until he can rise above the narrow confines of his individualistic concerns to the broader concerns of all humanity".[67]

Warrior leaders rise above the narrowness of their own concerns to embrace the broader concerns of the whole of humanity. In our current world, would you or would you not – at least instinctively – call them unreasonable? And would you also call them – essential?

Your reflection

Here are a few questions to reflect on:

1. What are the promises your own world can count on you for?
2. What's the place you are shaping your world from:
   conformity or integrity? How do you know?
3. What's the rebel within you that could be of service to your world?
4. What else requires you to pause and reflect?

CHAPTER 8: The Voice

ALL TOO OFTEN we are the players in a game in which our choice differs from rising above the narrow confines of our individualistic concerns to what concerns us all. The examples that prove this range from the painful episodes in our collective history to the smallest-scale events in our organisations, communities and families. What may be hard to accept is the notion that we all collectively contribute to such situations when we, instead of speaking up, choose to bring silence justified by a simple belief that says: my voice does not matter.

Embracing this feeling of powerlessness is so inviting because the short-term personal safety feels so much more reasonable than what we know may be collectively needed in the long run. We have witnessed or experienced challenging situations already and so we know that to speak is to risk. We don't speak, we don't run a risk – our world has trained us well. It has tamed us.

And yet, bold leaders refuse to be tamed. They speak up in the culture of silence even when it's most risky. Rather than embracing powerlessness, they know that their opinion matters. When it takes shape in their words, when it's given their voice, their leadership actually comes to life.

For their leadership to come to life by using their voice, bold leaders need to listen first. They listen for the unspoken, for what's there and matters but is not being said or heard, just to be able to give it a voice and invite others to do the same.

It's irrelevant whether it starts with what's unspoken in their teams, their entire organisations, their other communities or any other aspect of their world. It does not matter whether by speaking up they attempt to change the world or how things are in the smallest project of their team that year. Bold leaders address the unspoken issues and, going beyond sorting out the current situation, they elevate the conversation to the bigger, bolder level at which everyone says what needs to be said and hears what needs to be heard. It's the level that makes change not only possible, but also very much real.

To be able to create such a contribution, in the core of their leadership bold leaders nurture the belief that all voices matter, and they readily hold this belief in all its discomfort.

Unspoken

The land of the unspoken is built by all of us keeping quiet, and that leads everyone to a whole wide world of assumptions – the unsaid messages unconsciously but strongly nurtured within. If what we voice powerfully shapes our outer reality, then what we silently assume within does it just the same to the reality within us. In fact, what I dare to know is that we have all experienced at some point in our lives how what's not being said gradually becomes heard even louder in both our inner and our outer world.

The sound of the unspoken is loud everywhere, and sometimes particularly loud in our organisations. We need to be clear on the fact that what's not being talked about in our workplace designs our life there even more than what *is*. Everything that continues to be unspoken is costing the organisations a great deal of what most impacts the success and the image of their brand, and that is the meaningful engagement of their employees.

Not being talked about

"It's just driving me crazy."

"What's **it***?" I asked.*

"It's them!" she shouted, referring to her management board colleagues. "It's how they don't want to openly talk about it, how they are presenting the story for others in the organisation when we all know that no one believes it. They don't believe in their own story!" She raised her voice angrily before she continued: "I can understand that they've got no other way, I mean we haven't got much choice... apparently, but still...", and then she stopped for a second as her anger almost became sadness, "...still we can name it among ourselves. I'm not being irrational or business unsavvy. But we can say it the way it is. The way we all know it is."

What was really driving her crazy was the unspoken that lived in the system. The unspoken that she clearly felt was present but not voiced. In her view, management refused to let it be voiced.

"What's your question for them?" I started pointing her to her bold voice.

"What's **my question** *for them?" She sounded as if she had just heard something that did not make much sense to her.*

"Yes," I said and added, "in fact, let me tweak that a little bit: What's **your** *question for* **all of you***?"*

She paused as if allowing it to land within her. "My question for all of us." She made it sound like a statement at first. And then, with another breath, she started opening up to the invitation of her currently challenging business reality: "Here's my question for all of us. What could become different for us if we just had an open conversation about how we're being forced to implement something that goes so strongly against our values? Because we all know that this is exactly what's happening. What would change among us if we courageously put this topic on the table? It's not about sorting it out, it's not that simple or linear."

"What is it about then?" I was curious.

"It's about restoring trust among ourselves through a transparent conversation, through saying it the way it is. And it's about the possibility of handling the situation differently with our trust restored and our integrity honoured."

I nodded in support of her insight. "And you – if you initiate that conversation, how will that change you?" I smiled, curious.

She looked at me and said: "You know, speaking up excites me and scares me at the same time." And then she continued through a joyful laugh: "Oh, I just remembered what we once said. Excitement and fear stand for a place where all the important stuff begins."

When people can't speak or at least they assume they can't, they lose meaning. Because when they can't speak, it is as if they are not allowed to express, to question, to explore, to seek. What's taken away from them is the possibility of being seen and heard in what matters to them, to share important parts of themselves and their meaning-making of the world, to co-create with others from the reality that is emerging in parallel with their voice. This absence of conversation is in fact the absence of people's creative participation, the absence of their engagement.

In his book *Radical Wholeness: The Embodied Present and the Ordinary Grace of Being*, Philip Shepherd[68] talks about how different cultures recognise different senses. While the Western culture has been taught to have five senses – touch, taste, smell, hearing and sight – the Anlo-Ewe culture of West Africa understands senses in a different way. And so, in their culture, they consider speech to be one of the senses that they use to discover their way forward.

Just like they would use their hands and the sense of touch to move through physical space.

This concept offers a hugely important distinction of speech being a means of – as Shepherd says – discovery rather than delivery. I see this being aligned with the belief that true wisdom lies not in the right answer as much as it does in the right question. We could say that the purpose of our speaking is to open up the conversation and not to serve a predefined fixed opinion to the table, requiring others to receive it in submission.

If bold leaders have any sixth sense, I believe it is the sense of speech. Their work is to honour speaking and listening in every context. They don't speak to state what they know. They speak to name what's known to everybody but which nobody dares to say. They speak to seek what's needed next for everyone. They dare to know what matters, but they don't claim to be right. Rather than explaining their assumptions in an attempt to make them legitimate, they explore them just to be able to clear them and leave space for diversity of perspectives. For whatever else needs to be said and heard.

Bold leaders create from the unspoken. Tuning in to their environment – awake and in service – they recognise what matters most, and hold their concern as their ally in hearing the unspoken loud and clear to be able to give space to its voice.

As they do so, what really gives space to their leadership voice is the spaciousness of their mind. That means an expanded consciousness through which they clearly see their concern and their power as equals and are firmly convinced that all voices need to be heard to reveal the unspoken. Holding that conviction in the spaciousness of their mind, they don't just believe that their voice matters. They believe that all voices matter and that makes all the difference to their leadership.

What they are being guided by in this process is questions more than answers: What's unspoken and wanting to be named and put on the table? What's our silence saying that we aren't? What's that conversation we all need to be engaged in now? Because if we don't, what happens then? Who else needs to speak, who else needs to be heard? And then who else?

They are consciously guided by these questions even when it's most risky, staying true to their work even more so in a culture of silence. Because when they speak, rising above the inward-looking concerns to the common good, they come alive and empower others to come alive too through using their voice in the face of this risk for that which matters most.

The true empowerment, therefore, comes as a reward from stepping into the fire and being willing to stay with and in discomfort. The discomfort – that beautiful hot seat calling for a bold leader.

Seated in the midst of fire

The truth is that we can all be that leader seated in the midst of fire. The reality is that not everyone dares to embrace that role because it is a place of discomfort.

There's another subtle difference in the way this opportunity is perceived. Rather than a role, bold leaders consider embracing the discomfort to be their work. It is what they are here to do. It is when they are making a difference. It is how they are creating their contribution.

Bold leaders pursue what deeply matters to them, despite the uncomfortable presence of fear or risk. Contrary to attempts to avoid those feelings and eliminate discomfort, to be able to move on in their endeavours, bold leaders have the capacity to stay with that state. They stay in the uncomfortable emotional space, conditioning themselves to be daring on their deepest human level, on the level of their soul.

This is their readiness to simultaneously hold both their vision and the discomfort: the vision of how the world could look in the future and the discomfort of how it feels right now also because they have dared to act. It's an edgy and uncontrollable context. It is also the context in which bold leaders make pursuing that vision for the better future of whatever small or broad issue more important than having a short-term feeling of comfort and control.

By holding the vision and the discomfort, bold leaders lead at the edge of the confrontation, always and with everyone, themselves included. They are uncomfortably seated in the midst of fire. At this point, there are at least two legitimate questions to be asked. Why would bold leaders willingly sit in the fire?[69] And how do they do that?

I've partially answered the why question – because they cannot not. It's their work. It is what life expects of them and meeting that expectation is where they find their meaning. The nature of life is to grow and so the only thing we are truly meant to do in our lifetime is to live that nature of life and grow. Everything else is stories we construct around that one human mission. Growth is the essence of everything and often it starts by us taking a seat in the middle of the fire.

From this perspective, by taking that seat, we go beyond merely handling the situation. We lift, expand and deepen the growing conversation in which everyone has something to say and something to hear. We do it to allow for a change to happen because change loves such spacious conversation.

So how do those bold leaders stay in that space?

Leadership is an intentional sport that cannot be played well unconsciously. Earlier in this book I spoke about leaders' task to choose their intentions, their approach or metaskill as a "come from place" in their leadership. In more practical language, it is a decision you make about how you are going to be in what you are about to do. That decision defines your presence regardless of the arising circumstances. You choose your response from how you've decided to be instead of reacting unconsciously. That, already, is the beginning of discomfort.

Part of my practice includes doing Organisation and Relationship Systems Coaching. The reality of that work is that we as coaches often have to hold a lot of discomfort while meeting the systems – teams, families or partnerships. Meeting them in their confronting space requires from us that we handle the discomfort consciously and choose our intentions carefully, the metaskills with which we approach them.

While the metaskills can be different depending on the context, even changed in the middle of a meeting as we respond to what those systems may need in the moment, I've realised that three of them are my best allies in holding the discomfort as I'm seated in the midst of fire. I believe they can be well applied to anyone using their voice in their leadership to initiate uncomfortable conversations.

The first one is ***unfolding the unspoken***. There is something unspoken in every system, something that is not being said or heard and as such is – figuratively speaking – colouring the walls of the room and impacting how it feels to be in it.

Bold leaders' intention is to always enable the unspoken to unfold because that's what changes the colours of the walls in the room. Before it starts unfolding, its existence needs to be revealed or – to be more precise – someone, some bold leader needs to name the elephant in the room, that metaphorical creature visible to everyone, but nameable often only by a few. As we name it and reveal the unspoken, the emotional shift happens; suddenly it's no longer the shade of oppression or control and command, but rather the colours of freedom, authenticity, the space in which people are being heard and seen by invitation. The space in which everyone is invited to speak and listen.

The essence of this approach is to enable everyone to say what needs to be said and equally enable them to hear what needs to be heard. Holding the metaskill of unfolding the unspoken while being in conversation with others means being open to hear all the voices, even the ones that seemingly carry the least importance because they are all needed for two things to be understood: first, what is happening within the system now, and second, what wants to happen next.

Unfolding the unspoken is easier said than done. Depending on their formal position and history of experience, there are always people within the system thinking that either speaking or hearing is far too risky, too uncomfortable. When that is identified, we've found the place where we need a bold leader to invite all voices in and, committed to sit in the midst of fire, facilitate the unlocking of the individual and collective potential as the so far unspoken begins to unfold.

The second one is ***love***. As the unspoken begins to unfold, what we need lots of is – love. Regardless of how you decide to define this word for yourself – understanding, compassion, support or other – know that love ensures that the potentially heated confrontation stays creative instead of being turned into a reactive conflict.

Unfolding the unspoken initiates the change. And people naturally resist change, experiencing it as an edge that they need to cross. Bold leaders help others cross their edge. The edge of fear, the edge of risk, the edge of losing whatever they feel they don't want to let go of to let the change come in. Instead of judging their pace and their attitude towards the change, bold leaders choose to boldly and committedly love others over the edge despite the heat of the situation and their personal involvement in it.

The third metaskill is ***bolder conversation***. Everything that's unspoken is in fact a bolder conversation waiting to be initiated. What that also means is that bolder conversations start by listening first.

Once they develop, bolder conversations are never about who's right and who's wrong. That's not a bolder conversation but rather a closed limiting talk, and it could well be a monologue rather than a conversation. Bolder conversations are about what is and what's next for whoever is engaging in them. As such, they are often non-linear, uncontrolled, complex and emotional. They are simultaneously uncomfortable and potentially the most important ones we could be having in that moment to create the change that matters.

We could all find a seat in the fire in any area of our life and work that is – more or less patiently – waiting to be occupied by someone. Why not by us? I believe that the perspective of the heated seat changes drastically as we apply this intentional approach to any situation: unfolding the unspoken on the wings of fierce love and to the spaciousness of a bolder conversation.

That is how bold leaders lead in important situations. This approach does not make these situations any more comfortable. That's not in bold leaders' focus, as the aim of bringing their voice is not to honour comfort. The aim is to eventually honour growth.

Bolder conversation

As well as always being in a relationship, we are always in a conversation. There are two types of conversation that all of us are in, at all times. One of those conversations is the internal one that happens with ourselves in our own heads. The other one is the conversation that happens with others. Both can be daring or not, making us and our work in our lifetime somewhat bigger or smaller by choice.

In bold leadership everything leads to a bolder conversation with oneself and others. If you are not able to open up a bolder conversation with yourself, you probably won't be able to initiate a real bold one with others either. Building the muscle for initiating bolder conversations is a development journey that – just like any other – starts with the willingness to learn, unlearn and relearn.

The first thing that bold leaders learn is that the conversations are designing their life and work. What they are saying to themselves and others defines the quality of the life they live and the work they do. What they keep unspoken does so too.

If we take this concept to the context of the organisations, as we did earlier with the unspoken, we can say that the conversations are designing your life in your workplace. What's being talked about, and even more so what's *not* being talked about, is costing your organisation success and your employees the culture they desire to experience in order to be meaningfully engaged in their work.

Bold leaders open up and hold bolder conversations for better organisations, the ones that nurture a culture that everyone wants to work in and be in. In my work I hear too many employees saying that they want a better culture in teams or organisations that they work in. The very same message often comes from their leaders as well, making it sound as if they are once again collectively creating an atmosphere that they collectively don't want.

Your workplace conversations are designing your culture right now, at the moment of you reading this. Without speculating on the details of the culture your people would want to work in, let's open up a conversation about how you – as bold leaders – could create the culture that human nature would collectively desire and what your role is in supporting it to become reality in whatever your specific context is.

Creating such a culture is a conversation about learning and embracing these five perspectives:

1. Bold leaders activate leadership in everyone: themselves and others. They start doing this by believing that all voices matter.
2. Bold leaders are great coaches who support people's passions.
3. Bold leaders are initiators of better and bolder conversations that get created from whatever is unspoken.
4. Bold leaders bring their integrity to work to create safety in the workplace so that these conversations can actually happen.
5. Bold leaders' legacy is creative thinking and meaningful talking kept alive in their organisation long after they're gone.

In addition to learning new things, developing the ability to initiate bolder conversations requires leaders to unlearn the old ways of being and doing and learn a few new ones. In my experience, distinctions are a very powerful tool so let's address the three important ones that will show us what we actually need to learn and unlearn for initiating bolder conversations.

The most essential distinction bold leaders need to be aware of is that between ***having advice and having a voice***. The key difference between these two is that having advice for someone keeps us safe. We're telling others what they should do and we're doing it from a safely protected distance, not stepping into the fire ourselves. Contrary to that, having a voice is automatically engaging us, involving us in the matter of things. We care enough to speak up, we're part of it, it concerns us. It matters to us enough to step up and expose ourselves to the risk. We boldly speak *to* it as opposed to safely talking *about* it. We are seated in the midst of the fire. Again, by choice.

The second important distinction is the one between ***controlling and creating***. Bold leaders hold the belief that true leadership is a risk and that there's no such thing as safe leadership other than an illusion of it. We all want to be a part of something bigger, but we want a safe way to achieve that. Safe leadership is controlling, avoiding failure. Bold leadership is creating, shaping a legacy that matters. And that legacy is, to say the least, creative thinking and bolder conversations that remain embedded in the culture even when the leader is no longer there. Creating that legacy requires bold leaders to not stay silent so as to control what they personally feel they have in that very moment. It requires them to bring their voice and speak up in order to create what they know is missing in their world. The new possible that depends on us voicing it out.

The third distinction that bold leaders need to be familiar with to do their work of initiating bolder conversations is the distinction between ***being knowers and being learners***. Having to know the right answer will most likely close any potential for conversation as well as impose a huge pressure to be perfect in one's righteousness. That's not what the bolder conversations are about. Instead of that, they are the opportunity for joint learning. They are the new possible that we are discovering together. The only thing we need to know is that the bolder we show up in them, the bigger they will be for all of us, designing our reality in a better, more meaningful way. Bolder conversations are our joint way of inheriting the new possible instead of remaining stuck in the outdated mindset that no longer serves our reality.

In addition to learning and unlearning, there is a statement that bold leaders need to relearn over and over again: bold leaders' work is to activate leadership in everyone, in themselves and in others.

They do so by initiating bigger, better and bolder conversations that start with the unspoken, but end with a loud and clear voice that cuts through discomfort and asks: What's next for us? What are we ready for now that we were not ready for before? How will our world see that we're ready; what is it that they will see us doing? What happens if we fail? What else do we need to say and hear to access the new possible that we've just created?

Bold leadership requires your voice to be heard. Truly bold leaders dare to speak up and when they do, they come alive and they empower others to their aliveness as well.

Often our leadership can be best measured by the outcome of the battle between our big heart and our bright head. If you just for a moment think of the position of these two body parts, you'll realise that right in the middle of those two key points is a place that generates our own voice. We have it for a reason and it's our task to find our way to express it.

Your reflection

Here are a few questions to reflect on:

1. What has been unspoken in your environment for too long? How is it inviting you to act? If you do, what will change?

2. What is the fire you are avoiding sitting in the middle of? What makes it important that you do step into it? What do you need to believe about yourself and others to be able to hold the discomfort of it?

3. How is the conversation you're having with yourself designing your life and work? How about the one you're having with others? What needs to change?

4. How is your voice shaping your bold leadership? How are you using it to activate leadership in others?

5. What in your life and work is worth your initiating a better, bigger and bolder conversation now, despite all the risk? What is that conversation?

6. What else requires you to pause and reflect?

CHAPTER 9: The Contribution

WHATEVER WE CHOOSE to show our interest for, whatever we choose to speak up for or stay silent about, stands for our contribution to the world. It stands for our leadership. And the way we bring our leadership to our world is shaping the contribution we are creating.

Our contribution does not recognise and neither does it depend on our formal authority. If we waited to be in a position of formal authority just to offer our contribution to our world, we would deny ourselves our natural human creative role and deprive our world of many important initiatives born out of our boldness. We would go against one of the most essential beliefs of bold leaders, saying that it is our concern and not our power that makes it possible for us to act.

In the end, leadership is acting on things that matter. It is this acting that creates contribution. In between the formal authority position granted and labelled "leader" and a secretly thought opinion about what really matters being said and done lies a space. That space is your leadership playground. The game you choose to play in that playground defines your leadership. Whether you choose it intentionally or non-intentionally, it will still define your leadership, and your leadership defines your contribution, that difference that you do or do not eventually make.

Non-authority leadership

In his book *Leadership Without Easy Answers*, Ronald Heifetz speaks about the impact of leaders who had no formal authority just eventually being given an informal one. These are people like Martin Luther King Jr. or Gandhi who, as Heifetz says, "push us to clarify our values, face hard realities, and seize new possibilities, however frightening they may be".[70]

It would be wrong to think that we do not need the impact that we connect with such people on many occasions in our everyday life, just as it would be wrong to think that we cannot have that sort of an impact ourselves, should we choose to act as leaders on those many occasions. If, because of the magnitude of their contribution to the world, this sounds ridiculous, I invite you to think about the situations in your organisation, your team, your community or family that stand for an opportunity for you to push others to do exactly what Heifetz talks about – clarify their values, face difficult events or truths, and take new exciting and scary possibilities. I dare to know that these situations represent the opportunity for you to do exactly the same for yourself.

The opportunities for us to act as leaders are everywhere. Positions of formal authority are scarce compared to the number of these opportunities. Luckily, we do not depend on them to exercise our true and bold leadership. Our contribution in the form of our leadership depends solely on our concern, and our bold choice to act upon it.

The practice of questioning

Another important practice in creating our leadership contribution is the practice of continuously questioning things in our world. Bold leaders are awake to what is happening in and around them and they nurture the practice of questioning everything as they search for new possibilities, for new truth.

"If you would be a real seeker after truth, it is necessary that at least once in your life you doubt, as far as possible, all things."[71] Bold leaders doubt continuously by pausing to question what happens in the dynamics between them and their environment, to hear what is collectively asked for, be it spoken or unspoken, to notice the journey we are collectively travelling with or without intention. They pause to question where our world is and where we are collectively taking it as a result of our leadership. Their practice of questioning is the expression of their responsibility for the world they are creating for both present and future generations.

This practice requires two things: a continuous curiosity and an eager readiness to pause and reflect. Many leaders will ask this important question from the perspective of their business realities: How do I find the time and motivation to pause and simply reflect in such a speedy pragmatic world?

Many organisational leaders resist the reflection work that is deep and slow in its essence partially because as such it is in direct conflict with the imposed imperative of their overpacked business realities which require a quick and practical solution to many real things. They don't have time and they want something fast so they can move on with (what they call) their real work. Rather than approaching things with lasting curiosity and reflection, their approach is the search for practical and pragmatic solutions.

In such a context, what they call their real work is of a very tactical nature. And as much as reality imposes the need to be tactical, that's not the essence of leadership. The essence of leadership is vision. Vision is not born out of tactics. Tactics do not generate vision, but follow it. And vision requires leaders to continuously question everything by using many of their intelligence centres: their head, heart and guts, their bodies, their souls. It requires them to question the existing and sense the emerging, the new possible. It is a matter of going deeper, and not necessarily faster.

This going deeper can also be called stillness. And so, questioning happens in the stillness of the mind, in moments of withdrawal. It happens in moments of a personal retreat where we face the question of the need we sense inside and the need we notice outside and the question of where these two collide. The point of collision is an invitation for our leadership, our contribution.

At this point it is important to differentiate leadership as merely acting and leadership as acting on the things that matter most. It is the latter that helps us to create our most important contribution through our intentional action towards our vision.

Here's what is important about leadership being visionary and intentional rather than tactical: shaping the world with our intentional leadership is what we are responsible for towards everyone that is here now and that will arrive in the future. What we – as bold leaders – owe ourselves and everyone is to continuously hold present one question: How does what I am deciding to do today create our world of tomorrow? Having that question embedded in all your leadership choices is a really bold practice of questioning.

Holding that question is a real imperative and an even more real challenge that the complexity of the current world imposes on leaders through a continuous whisper. Those who pause can hear that whispering voice better.

Power and wisdom gap

In my own leadership development journey, I've been very much inspired by the book *Presence: Exploring Profound Change in People, Organizations and Society.*[72]

In it, the so-called gap between our power and our wisdom is addressed. The topic is presented by quoting a UN senior officer closing his speech at the International Institute for Applied Systems Analysis in Austria with the following message: "I've dealt with many different problems around the world, and I've concluded that there is only one real problem: over the past hundred years, the power that technology has given us has grown beyond anyone's wildest imagination, but our wisdom has not. If the gap between our power and our wisdom is not redressed soon, I don't have much hope for our prospects."[73]

Despite its potential and unlike the power given to us by the technology we have developed, our wisdom has not grown beyond our wildest imagination. We have not been growing it. In the broadest possible sense, our boldest leadership contribution to our world is to stop failing at this task by intentionally redressing the gap between our power and our wisdom.

This gap is visible on many levels in our communities. It is very much there. It's only a matter of us pausing to raise our awareness of its existence.

Let's start with the family environment. With full respect to our different values, it is hard to find a family system today in which technology has not replaced a simple connecting human conversation to at least some extent. Let us go to a very practical level here: How many times do we answer the phone during a family lunch, willingly exchanging our human connection time with prioritised work productivity? Or perhaps taking the line of least resistance to handle different system needs, how often do we put a screen into our children's hands just to have peace and quiet over our meal? We may still sit in a circle together sharing food, with no actual connection shared among us.

Whatever the scenario is in your reality, this has become one of the hard truths: every single person in our closest community, regardless of their age, has their own piece of technology to connect with. The connection to this technology aims to replace the connection with a human being, with another person or even with ourselves. Here's another quote, this time by French scientist and writer Blaise Pascal, that if read carefully could be understood as an announcement of the power-wisdom gap: "All of humanity's problems stem from man's inability to sit quietly in a room alone." We can – to put it ironically – just give ourselves an interactive screen.

And now let's move this gap into the business environment. Working with a high-level team in the IT industry a few years ago, I was inspired by one of their closing comments after a two-day-long experiential workshop: "We now understand that we'll have to parallelly transform ourselves as people and our business and we'll have to keep doing it at all times." Just a few months after that, I was attending a round table on the topic of growing the economy in the tourism industry when the moderator sent this message almost out of nowhere: "May we never stop reminding ourselves that the development of humans comes first, and the development of things second."

You can debate which one of these is closer to your image of what the development needs to look like. This is what I choose to believe: it is our leadership imperative to lead business and human development in parallel, always putting the former in service of the latter.

In their book *An Everyone Culture: Becoming a Deliberately Developmental Organization*, Robert Kegan and Lisa Laskow Lahey describe the development of business potential and human potential as two halves of the same whole.[74] If we neglect the development of human potential, we create a space for something that the authors call the second job that everyone diligently performs but no one gets paid for: endless efforts to manage other people's impressions about them while hiding their own weaknesses. While they are occupied doing that, the exploration and the development of their own genuine wisdom suffers. The book shows us how there can be a very different scenario: a workplace in which people together with their payroll also receive meaning through their own individual and collective growth. Such workplaces, called deliberately developmental organisations, actively hold a radical belief that they will truly prosper by operating in deep alignment with what represents people's strongest motive for engagement – their growth.

It looks like these organisations are wholeheartedly and actively nurturing people's deepest development rather than inviting them to hide their natural wisdom and be simply intelligent instead. Because being simply intelligent seems to be more functional, more pragmatic in the world that's set up the way it is, which is to honour results as an expression of much desired productivity and efficiency, and human beings only as means to an end. Is there a better way to deepen the gap between our power and our wisdom on the most practical level?

Just like deliberately developmental organisations, we can start creating a different scenario today and every day ahead. In fact, it is exactly the path these organisations are already walking. We need to learn and we need to do it individually and collectively.

Learning plays a key role in starting to redress this so-called power-wisdom gap. If we're not willing to get in touch with our own humanity through committed self-development, we won't be able to spot a need for it on a larger scale. In the organisational context, if we're not willing to see that a collectively learning culture is an essential facet of overall business success, no strategy that we choose to apply for a successful business will live up to its full potential. It may generate success, but not to its fullest potential and not in the service of humanity. If that is your choice as a leader, you may as well name it.

To progress towards the changed world, we need to honour a disciplined individual and collective leadership learning practice amidst the overpacked business realities and in the face of the need for instant functionality. It must be rooted in our understanding that our wisdom is our key power and our culture is our most successful strategy. The culture that only feels as if it is being designed by other people, while in fact it's being designed by us every day, with every choice we make. Our every choice to question, to speak up, to try and change, or to give up is exactly what transforms - or not - our worlds into truly sustainable and meaningful communities.

It's not unreasonable to think that it's possible to live and work this way. It is consciously bold. And conscious boldness is what we need to close the gap between the power that technology has given us and our genuine human wisdom that serves our humanity. We can call it the process of healing. Or the process of refinding meaning.

The idea of closing the power-wisdom gap can be overwhelming because it almost requires the entire world to change. Our world culture to change. And culture from the systemic perspective behaves like a huge elephant with so many heavy body parts, so much effort needed for its tiny little movements. So, how do we do it?

We do it by welcoming daring enquiry rather than safe instructions. Because our bold leadership is defined by the questions that we dare to ask and stay with, and not by our addiction to the right answers.

So, welcome the conversation. Use your bold voice. Keep speaking up despite discomfort. Keep questioning. Keep connecting to yourself and other human beings, creating circles, metaphorically or literally, only to keep initiating bolder conversations. Keep doing it for whichever aspect of your world, in whatever group of people, speaking the truth to any power, and naming the elephant in the room. And the elephant will move.

I'm inviting you, as bold leaders, to pause and reflect on where the gap between power and wisdom exists in your universe. Where in your organisations, your communities, families, any of your worlds could you create your contribution by attempting to close it? Where could you start speaking the truth you sense is needed? What's the conversation you must not leave unopen based on even your intuitive concern? Where is your voice called for? And how are you choosing to answer that invitation?

In the end, the legacy you create, your work that carries the most meaning for your world, depends on your capability to recognise and your choice to answer the many invitations along the way.

I believe that the realm of ***Universe*** is central to one's bold leadership in terms of the fact that both ***Self*** and ***Other*** are just leading us to this point in which we become very much awake and ready to be of service to whatever is larger than us. They are guiding us to the point where we start transforming our concern into our contribution to actually bring our leadership to the world in the service of change. To bring our leadership to that one Home we share together, one Universe.

Joseph Jaworski's book, *Source: The Inner Path of Knowledge Creation*, offers four principles at the very beginning, all of which refer to the concept of the universe. One of the principles will tell you that "everything in the universe, including human intentions and ways of being, affects everything else, because everything is part of the same unbroken whole".[75]

He also speaks about what he calls "Stage IV" leaders who are servant leaders developed to the next more comprehensive level. These leaders "combine their cognitive understanding of the world around them with a strong personal sense of possibility – the possibility of actualizing hidden potentials lying dormant in the universe, a view that carries with it the power to change the world as we know it".[76]

I am referring to Jaworski's work as my own inspiration of what leadership can be. It's up to you to explore his or any other work further and, as I said in the beginning, eventually choose the level to which you wish to understand the name of this part of the book, the term ***Universe***, as a realm of your own leadership.

In whatever way you decide to understand the magnitude and nature of this term, my longing for you, and therefore for all of us, is that we experience it as an awakening of our strong personal sense of accountability, empowerment, hope and joy in co-creating a needed change in any aspect of our world. The awakening of our bold leadership to change any game.

Your reflection

Here are a few questions to reflect on:

1. What are you questioning in your world? What's your underlying concern? How does it shape your contribution?

2. In which aspect of your reality are you aware of the power-wisdom gap? What is your leadership response to it?

3. What else requires you to pause and reflect?

Before proceeding to Part 4, here's an invitation for you:

Great leaders initiate bolder conversations. They say what needs to be said and hear what needs to be heard.

Visit www.boldleadership-culture.com and schedule a strategy call with me to discuss how to bring the **Organisation and Relationship Systems Coaching** to your organisation and teach your leaders how to boldly lead their teams by radically changing the conversation.

PART 4
LEGACY

It is the daring – and not necessarily the knowing – that enables us to change any game.

The work you love

William James, known as the father of American psychology, said that the great use of life is to spend it on something that will outlast it. Work that outlasts life is a wonderful definition of legacy. What I also believe to be an equally amazing perspective of legacy is the work that you actually – live and love.

Every person leaves a legacy. To deny that would mean denying the natural human ability to create. In fact, I believe that human beings are a legacy per se as there is no person who hasn't touched someone else's life in some way at least once in their lifetime. We all leave a legacy in the form of our impact on others.

While we all have an impact on some or on many people with the way we live and lead, I'd like to initiate a conversation about our leadership as an opportunity to create our legacy in the most conscious way. In the context of leadership and legacy, the first question leaders need to ask themselves about who they are and what they do is this: Am I making a living or am I leaving a legacy? While both are absolutely legitimate choices in one's life, the latter is undoubtedly much closer to the perspective of bold leaders doing the work they love.

Leaders who are consciously leading from ***Self***, ***Other***, and ***Universe***, bringing the full capacity of their soul to these realms of leadership, naturally arrive at the point of creating a legacy. It's impossible that they bring themselves all-in to these realms without at least starting to understand what their meaningful work is and feeling the readiness to bring it out there in service of the world. And that's what legacy actually is: something that gets consciously created out of our meaningful work – the work that is ours to do in our lifetime and in service of our world. Notice the depth and width of this concept as opposed to just doing the work to make a living.

Defined as a process, leadership in the realm of ***Legacy*** means three things: first, discovering what your meaningful work is; second, being unshakeably committed to do that work throughout all life's discomforts, and third, playing big in that work in service of your world.

Our work, the one we are here to do, has an inevitable potential to outlast our life. What it requires of us and our leadership is to keep seeking it, exploring and rediscovering whatever has a larger meaning for us. You can call it a purpose. In my view, it is far less important how you decide to name it than how you learn to recognise it. And you'll recognise it by the way it pulls you to itself, grabs the attention of your mind and gets hold of your heart centred in the middle of your soul. Perhaps you can call it a passion. Or simply – love. Whatever it is that you decide to call it, you'll recognise it by the fact that it makes you feel alive.

The second important thing in creating a conscious legacy is our commitment, our dedication to the work we are here to do. Our commitment is visible in our choices. There are three important ones we need to stay committed to in creating our legacy: our choice to express our passion, our choice to always act from integrity, and our choice to be bold in repeatedly prioritising those first two, despite all obstacles in our life and our leadership. In other words, our decision to engage our passion, our integrity and our boldness is what to a large extent transforms our leadership into our legacy. Making that decision is a challenge in a world that most of the time tries to compress your passions that give meaning to your life in exchange for giving larger space to your feeling of safety.

The third imperative in consciously creating our legacy is to do our meaningful work in service of our world, whatever our world may be. Leadership starts, but does not end with Self. It is not a lonely game, no matter how much some systems strive to convince us of that. Equally, our legacy starts with our own meaningful work but that work is a means to an end and not an end in itself. Your meaningful work is what you are making a lasting difference with in your environment, regardless of how big or small that environment is. Rather than being about how big your world is, it is about how much your meaningful work is needed, desired and meaningful for others too.

Discovering your meaningful work starts with the awareness of what your soul desires. Nurturing those desires means feeding love to our dreams as opposed to suppressing the hunger of our insatiable fears. We will never liberate ourselves from the fear; that's human nature. We're merely left to shift the focus. And so, when it comes to pursuing our meaningful work and creating our legacy, fears are not our focus, but merely an indication of the importance and intensity of our love for something.

Legacy can be generally defined as the way we live and lead, the way we make choices and create experiences in our life and our leadership, to those that matter to us and to the people who belong to our world. When I say this, I instantly recall *A Beautiful Mind* – the biographical film that tells us the story of the American mathematician John Forbes Nash, Jr. who received a Nobel Prize in economics for his work in game theory. We also learn that John Nash struggled with the severe mental illness of schizophrenia, as we follow the course of his extraordinary and meaningful life and work in this film based on Sylvia Nasar's bestselling book of the same title. Professor Nash's theories, widely used in economics, represent a very tangible legacy and that's a clear fact. Still, the film about his life and work leaves us with a very deep impression of the many other intangible legacies that this maths genius and the people who were part of his life have left. As we hear his speech while receiving the Nobel Prize in the final scene of the film, we are struck by his spouse Alicia's legacy of infinite love towards him and his own legacy of infinite will despite all his health challenges. Love and will. Compared to his influential work, these intangible legacies are just as real.

My parents are not Nobel Prize winners and they haven't changed the world on a large scale with their inventions or theories. What they have done amazingly, though, is created a legacy of determination and persistence that they have been instilling in me even before I was able to consciously recognise it. I'm questioning whether they do it consciously or not, but it does not matter to me. What matters to me is the message I see in everything they do, and the message says: whatever your life circumstances are, you always stand up and keep walking. Taking this energy of survivors, the energy of bold overcomers, and transforming it into the energy of a creator is what I see as part of my meaningful work. I thank my parents for their legacy that has helped me walk a good half of the way.

While being generated from our own soul desire, from what gives meaning to us, our conscious legacy is ultimately the creation of what's collectively meaningful, what brings meaningful change to any aspect of our world apart from ourselves. Sometimes, our work ends up having great proportions of collective meaning as important changes are created not only by us, but with us and through us. I believe that is the moment when we reach next level boldness in our leadership as real game changers, as big-hearted warrior disruptors crating legacy from one fundamental truth: the change that makes the world more human is always worth the risk.

CHAPTER 10: Meaningful Work

THE FAMOUS WORDS of Howard Washington Thurman, a philosopher, theologian and author with a leading role in many social justice movements of the twentieth century, were: "Don't ask what the world needs. Ask what makes you come alive, and go do it. Because what the world needs is people who have come alive."[77] Bold leaders come alive through the meaningful work they are here to do for their worlds.

So, what is it that the world needs?

It clearly needs people who are bold enough to search for what is meaningful to them so that they can create what is meaningful for their worlds. Bold leaders who know what they stand for and how what they stand for is serving their world.

Today's world glorifies speed, busyness, superficial and virtual experience, leaving us continuously paradoxically wondering what on earth happened with the truly empowered and deeply engaged individuals. In such a world, going deep to search for meaning looks like a rare heroic act. So rare that we forget the fact that we are first and foremost spiritual beings, fully empowered and authentically engaged only in the work that we find meaningful on our deepest level.

The world needs people who will boldly search for and be ready to discover what that meaningful work is on their deepest level regardless of the entry point through which they are invited to its discovery: their obvious talent, the pain that they have been through or simply their message created from any of their accumulated experiences that they feel must be voiced and shared in some form.

The world needs people who will firmly commit to what they've discovered to be their meaningful work in such a way that they cannot *not* choose it over and over again. Even as life seems to be pushing them in completely different directions, they stay committed to that force of meaning they are relentlessly being pulled by – their work they are here to do.

The world desperately needs those people who are ready to wholeheartedly engage in their meaningful work to initiate important change in their corner of the world.

The conversation about meaning

Viktor Frankl's[78] life and work teaches us about the human ability to search for meaning in the most inhuman circumstances. Through this man's courageous story, we get an almost palpable sense of what it feels like when someone finds meaning in the midst of the horror of their reality, to say the least. Meaning generates a sense of fulfilment in whatever course of events – a feeling of being deeply, wholly alive. In Frankl's context, it seemed to be a desire to ***stay*** alive because life has purpose; it has a larger meaning than its current circumstances. Do we really need better evidence of the empowering nature of meaning in life even in the midst of an indescribable experience of human misery?

When what we do makes deep sense to us, we are on purpose and we feel fulfilled. According to Frankl, the meaning of life is to find one's purpose, clarify one's "why" and take responsibility to act on it. What that "why" is, is an individual matter for all of us.

Richard Barrett[79], an author and internationally recognised thought leader on the evolution of human values in business and society, also speaks about the meaning of our human lives, saying that – as we experience our own reality

– we individually give a subjective meaning to our own existence. In that process, according to Barrett, our ego tries to justify our existence through its needs, and our soul knows why we exist. Its desire is to fully express its unique nature and talents through us. And so, what living a meaningful life is really about, is pursuing our passion that will help us discover our unique talents, perhaps also the ones that we may not even know we have.

While we all may be fond of different theories and conversations about meaning, one thing we do share: each of us is the seeker of meaning for our own life. It's up to us to ask and answer the question of why we exist.

Earlier in this book I spoke about the importance of the state of constant enquiry as part of everyone's personal leadership development path. This process starts with questions: What am I here for? What's the purpose of me being in this world? As we are developing within the SOUL framework from our deep self-reflection to our readiness to act in our world, our questions become a bit more focused: What's really my work? What do I need to do while I am here? These are the questions we need to answer for ourselves; there is no possibility of delegating the task of answering questions about the meaning of our life and work to anyone else. And neither can you delegate the task of asking them.

Let's take a closer look at what having your meaningful work as a leader actually is. On a high level, your meaningful work means that you have a vision you are ready to stand for. By pursuing it, you're also inspiring others to discover what they are ready to stand for, to create the vision that gives them and their worlds a deep sense of meaning and aliveness and as such is worth the risk.

How do we find our meaningful work? Probably the best answer lies in what was already mentioned earlier in this book: to go higher you must first go deeper. By deep learning about the way that you exist in relationship with yourself, with others and with your world. In the context of this book, by boldly exploring the SOUL framework, you recognise and answer the invitation to transform what gives most meaning to you into the vision that's meaningful for your world.

The entry point through which you are invited to the discovery of your meaningful work may vary. I like to differentiate three of them. People like artists, athletes or scientists may access it through their obvious talent. Others, perhaps through the painful experiences of difficulties or losses in their lives. Or some people simply recognise their inner message that has become clearer throughout their accumulated experience of different stories and they have to voice and share it in some form. There is a passion for something behind all these entry points. That passion is not a superficial drive for financial wealth, social status or other forms of recognition; it is rather our deeper desire to make a difference and realise the meaning for ourselves and others.

Let's be more granular in the definition of what meaningful work is. The meaningful work of a talented tennis player or a genius mathematician, rather than being understood as merely playing tennis or creating theories, is what they are evoking and changing in their worlds by using their obvious talents. Others will discover their talents along the process but theirs, as well, will just be a means to a higher end. The meaningful work of people who have gone through painful life experiences is not to simply overcome their pain, although that will be a natural step in the process, but to create from overcoming their pain so that it can heal their world too. Finally, there are people who have crystallised their opinions about what matters out of their different – not necessarily painful – experiences and their meaningful work is to transform them into important messages and actions for their world.

As always, there are very successful people so defined by social norms that they have not actually or at least not fully engaged in work that is meaningful for them. It must be possible, because if it wasn't so, we would not witness so many people labelled as successful and at the same time unfortunately coming across as unfulfilled and uninspiring. We are left to wonder how different, how much bolder and world-changing their impact would have been, had their work been meaningful for them.

If we wanted to explain leaders' meaningful work by means of creative leadership competencies, we could perhaps look at the dimension of Achieving[80] in the Leadership Circle Profile™[81], more precisely at the sub-dimension called Purposeful & Visionary[82]. As the definition of this sub-dimension states, by being purposeful and visionary, leaders have a deep sense of purpose visible in their optimism, enthusiasm, and passion: a compelling vision that they communicate to others, encouraging them to create their own. As this competency explains, the key contribution of leaders is to cultivate vision and purpose.

Scoring low on the Purposeful & Visionary dimension is an indication that leaders may be managing effectively but they are not leading. They are not showing up as leaders because they lack a sense of deep purpose and they lack vision. And vision – as the competency again teaches us – is largely synonymous with leadership itself.

Here's the way I see it: what makes us leaders is creating a conscious legacy from our meaningful work communicated and pursued through our vision. In the absence of the meaningful work, there is no leadership, no vision and consequently no consciously created legacy.

If the conversation about our meaningful work is a conversation about our deep sense of purpose and our vision, then it is also very much a conversation about our inspirational values. Because how passionate can our vision be, if it's not based on our most inspirational values? So, what sort of values generate our most compelling vision?

If what our ego needs is our fundamental values, those that generally speaking keep us safe, then what our soul desires are those that truly inspire our aliveness. They are the source of our deepest sense of fulfilment. And, as such, they have a request for us. They are asking us to discover them and choose them. In fact, they are asking us to keep rediscovering and rechoosing them as we navigate the complexity of our lives. Honour them in our integrity at all times. In other words, our soul requires our continuous presence, our wholeness and our boldness, and it promises to reward us with a fulfilled existence in return.

There is no end to the search for meaning of why we live and what our work is during our lifetime. Equally, there is no end to deepening the exploration of our values and noticing the variety of their expression at different stages of our lives.

If you met me as a ten-year-old girl and asked me what I wanted to be I would have first answered a surgeon and then a reporter. My idea of becoming a surgeon left me when I first watched a documentary on surgery on the internal organs. I haven't pursued the role of a reporter either. However, the key values that I imagined being honoured in both of these callings are still with me today.

I am honouring these values as a developmental coach and a writer: I support the development of people, I help them heal, I'm exposed to cultural diversity through my work, I listen to people's stories and I write about them through the lens of human development and a search for meaning. Not only am I honouring them in my day-to-day work, I also have a strong vision of how they can become an increasing part of my world and for what purpose, which for me defines the *what* and the *how* of my meaningful work in the long term.

Perhaps it's worth going back to your childhood dreams to collect the wisdom of that naturally curious being about what your meaningful work truly is.

The expression of our meaningful work can vary in the course of our life. Those key values underlying our work remain the same, giving it its meaning even when the circumstances drastically change.

When our work is meaningful, our life makes sense. We become alive and the world becomes a somewhat better place because of the aliveness we bring to it. So, referring again to Thurman's quote, the world needs many things, but that's not the thing. We are not all here with the task of addressing all of those things that the world needs, but each of us ***is*** here with the task of addressing some of our world's needs. When discovering our meaningful work that makes us come alive, we'll know which ones.

And then, as bold leaders, we'll take responsibility for our work.

Purposeful achievement

Meaningful work leads to purposeful achievements.

I believe there is way too much work in the world that does not carry our most inspirational values and too many people that have given up their natural human desire to have a vision in exchange for a purely operational life. I feel we have willingly imprisoned ourselves through our fundamental values that dictate the meaning of our work for us to be safe and nothing deeper than that. We do not go past that ego need and into the land of our soul desires. And neither do organisations, as our collective world, encourage us to take that path.

If we reduce the conversation about meaningful work to a very practical level, we may open up the topics of empowerment and engagement, both recurring topics in the organisational setting. Two very present and painful spots. What I have realised is that those who frequently search for a solution on how to empower and engage others are often little empowered and engaged themselves.

What that also means is that they are often in much need of redirecting their search to the existence of inspirational values within themselves. If they did that, I dare to know that they would stand a great chance of first empowering themselves for those types of achievements that could make the difference in organisations – the purposeful ones.

Stuck in a purposeless life

I remember hearing the sound of my own high heels, their click-clack down the building's cold corridor. I was walking towards the chairman's office with as little enthusiasm as possible. In that very moment I became aware of the sickness, a feeling of being completely fed up with playing this meaningless corporate role. As if the clatter of the heels revealed what had become the lifeless nature of my soul imprisoned in that fictitious world. The only thing is that it wasn't fiction, it was real and it felt so purposeless. My pain was real.

What also seemed very real was my fear-driven assumption that there was no life outside that world I would have loved to call fiction, and – to my horror – this assumption was gradually being transformed into a realisation that there was even less life within.

I have absolutely no recollection of why I was going to where I was, neither what date, year or time it was or for how long after that moment I remained part of that world. What I do remember all so vividly is the sound of my shoes, my dull grey skirt, my lifeless movements, and my self-talk: What am I learning? How on earth am I growing around here? I feel stuck in a meaningless moment lasting for so long that I cannot even remember any other taste of life. And wouldn't it be lovely to walk another corridor tomorrow, one in which there's creativity, ideas, opportunities to learn, possibilities to grow and create something meaningful together with other people? Something that makes sense! Wouldn't it be nice if I could just wake up in another company, another culture tomorrow? Is it too late? What if it isn't? Oh, if only I could walk another path tomorrow. And as I said that, I felt the thrill. I swear I felt it so real. This thrill of what I imagined to be a more meaningful reality.

I don't know what prompted this self-talk in that particular moment. By the time I got back from meeting the chairman, there was little space left in my head for thoughts about growth and meaning. That much I do remember. Still today, I am not able to contextualise this particular episode. But I am able to clearly recall the experience of it, all the way through my bones and into my soul.

Today as a coach I meet many such people lifelessly walking down their corporate corridors after they have been frantically running from one goal to another, making sure they overdeliver the work they actually find meaningless and exceed the expectations of someone who happens to feel deep down equally meaninglessly disengaged.

This is by no means everybody's story in the corporate setting. It is merely my belief that it is a frequent one. More frequent than we want it to be in the world that we say we collectively desire. And this story is systemically supported by organisations that seem to be nurturing productivity as opposed to purposeful achievement. Again, this is by no means an image of all organisations. My belief still is that it is a frequent one.

I all too often hear stories of people who do not find what they do in their organisations to be meaningful, aligned with their deepest values, or making sense for them as human beings. Many of them have even accepted the idea that asking for their work to be meaningful is an unrealistic request, an insane concept that won't get them too far in their careers. And so, they have given up this expectation. Under the influence of the particular culture and also the general organisational context, they have willingly stopped searching for the meaning behind their work, selling this natural human soul desire for a few ego incentives. It is what their organisations have taught them many times is realistic, reasonable and rewarded: delivery without questioning. And so, we end up finding our own little place under the sun with a life-long task to keep it at all cost, even after it has stopped making deep sense and started creating serious lifelessness.

And while some people run from one to another lifeless place under the sun that is much the same as the last, there are those who dare to open the conversation around what really matters. Their stories sound different.

Becoming a meaningful self

It was our fourth session. The face in front of me seemed to belong to a completely different person. It was no longer the face that was utterly tired, the face of someone who looked as though they had given up a million times already. No, this face was alive.

"You know what," she said, "I don't want this to simply be a change of job."

"What do you want it to be?" I asked.

"I want it to be a step closer to myself," she said, standing strong in her own empowerment.

"That sounds exciting, to say the least. I wonder what you actually mean by that?"

"What I mean is that I want to make a contribution. This is not just time to go to a similar position in the same industry. This is about achieving something more important than a higher pay-check or additional free time. It is about me bringing my strengths into creating something for others, something important, something that matters. Yes, this is about doing the work that matters. Isn't that what life is all about?"

"I surely believe it is," I said.

It was beautiful to walk by her side in the following few months and see her committedly mobilising herself to create and express what her soul needed, taking her time and keeping her focus, as she was becoming someone new through what made deep sense to her.

Here's what I truly believe about purposeful achievement: human beings are seekers of meaning. Their work must make sense for them to be authentically engaged. The exact meaning that we find and attribute to our life and work is an individual topic, but what we all have in common is the fact that having that sense of meaning is when we become empowered and engaged. It may start with our work, but this empowerment and engagement – or the lack of it for that matter – translates into the rest of our life as well.

Because they are accompanied by a sense of meaning, purposeful achievements are the antidote to the transactional contributions that we so often witness within organisations. This is how it usually sounds: what I get, is what I give. And the value of what I get develops a very fluctuating character over time as it depends on many things that I prioritise when I don't feel fulfilled by the meaningful nature of my work. There are many trade-offs that I prioritise when I do not prioritise meaning. This takes me to the following scenario: I live and I work, but I feel hardly alive and even less fulfilled as I'm choosing reasonable calculations over my natural core integrity.

Bold leaders do not settle for that. They refuse to stop questioning context that does not carry meaning. Because that is not collaboration, regardless of how much their organisational cultures want them to believe that's what it is; it is unquestioning submission. Not giving up the desire to have purposeful achievements created out of their meaningful work, they are shaping the world in a different way. A way that honours humans first and consequently witnesses far less mental illness and far more empowerment, authentic engagement and inspiring legacy.

Our world – whatever it is – is constantly being shaped, both the way we like it and the way we don't. And as much as we would sometimes like to think that this happens overnight, it doesn't. It happens in small steps, small bites, small acts of ours. Some of these small steps, long before our time, started to eliminate the search for meaning in many contexts of our life and work. Bit by bit. Until something else became the "normal" reality. There is no new normal and equally no old normal; there is always only the present normal. The one that is, that exists right now, is a result of somewhat smaller or bigger steps taken along the way. I believe there is not much use in looking back to explore how the present normal got created, as it's essential to look forward to what may be created in the future if we do not take that different small meaningful step right now. That's our bold leadership work now, in its broadest sense. And that will be our future conscious legacy that we owe to whoever is coming next.

Again, it is completely individual where we find most meaning. Whether it is in the opportunity to grow, to create, connect, or care, or perhaps all of them. Our meaningful work is ours to discover and follow. To better understand if you are on the path of your meaningful work, look for a gap between your sense of accomplishment and recognition and your sense of deep meaning and fulfilment. How does it feel to raise your own awareness of these distinctions? How does this gap feel, if there is one? And if you initiate a bolder conversation with yourself, what would you find out about it? What's there; what's missing, and what are you not daring to face?

By looking deeper into these questions, perhaps you'll be able to recognise those experiences in your organisations that you do not appreciate because they go against what your meaningful work actually is. They suffocate your passion and essentially go against your integrity and as such they are preventing your achievements from being grounded in your purpose.

There can be many reasons for you to tolerate this gap, and one secure outcome: a waste of your leadership legacy.

This gap is a conflict between pragmatic and visionary perspective: what the world is telling me that is realistic and reasonable and what I truly desire. If a leader's task is to close the gaps, this gap is only for the boldest of leaders. If you are a leader that wants to walk the path of achieving with purpose, you need to be one of them.

As a mother I often think about my son's future. Much to the despair of my motherly instincts, I know I cannot control it, so I'm left with my longings for him. And my longing for my currently six-year-old son is for him to get to know his meaningful passion. It is my belief that it will enable him to live a fulfilled life. Many would say this means being happy. But fulfilment is not always happiness. We witness that every day. In fact, what our children demonstrate so vividly to us is the instantly changeable character of happiness five minutes after they have received another toy or additional screen time. Or perhaps it's us after we've received another pay rise or a new role.

Unlike happiness that can end at any moment, fulfilment is a passion that gives deep sense to us and keeps us going forward feeling passionately alive. And while at some challenging life moments, it can feel no more solid than the fluctuating character of happiness, it is simply inviting us to keep rediscovering it because it represents the source of our truly meaningful work.

I long for my son, in whatever context he may find himself, to be bold enough to never leave that invitation unanswered.

Our soul's love

We all have our passions and we have them for a reason. The conversation about our passions is not the conversation about having them, it is the conversation about honouring them by choosing them as our work.

When we recognise our passion as our work and we choose to honour it, fulfilment is the only recognition we desire to receive. And rather than being happiness, this fulfilment stands for joy, for our deep sense of aliveness, for the force of meaning that we continue to be pulled by. Not driven. Invited by. Invited in such a way that we repeatedly cannot *not* accept it.

Once again, it is not a drive. It is love. Love is in the centre of our passion. And so, it all starts with love and us choosing it to be our force of creation of whatever matters in our world.

That potentially gives us the most accurate definition of meaningful work – our expression of the deepest love of our soul that we have the courage to keep choosing in service of our world.

Your reflection

Here are a few questions to reflect on:

1. What work is the source of deep meaning for you?
   How much of that work is there in your life?

2. What's fulfilling about your work achievements? What is not?

3. What are your strongest passions that go against your reasonable reality? Who would you become if you dared to pursue them? What difference would that make in your world?

4. What else requires you to pause and reflect?

CHAPTER 11:
The Commitment

THERE IS NO bigger waste of potential than discovering your meaningful work and not staying committed to it. Not only is that a huge waste of potential, it is also a betrayal of yourself and your world. Denying your passion that would serve your world is to deny your integrity.

Contrary to that, staying committed to what you have discovered to be your meaningful work means consistency and dedication to express it in whatever form. It means having a vision and travelling towards it regardless of the many discomforts of the journey. The more impossible it seems - or unreasonable and unrealistic - the more important it probably is.

The edgier it feels to express your meaningful work, the bigger its change potential is. And the world needs change. Corporate organisations, public services, health, educational, legal, political systems, governments, neighbourhood communities, families, so many corners of our world simply need change.

Initiating that change may well depend entirely upon your commitment to express your meaningful work.

The expression

There is no leadership legacy without expression. Your meaningful work cannot be transformed into your legacy without your willingness and dedication to express it. Keeping it for yourself is denying its contribution to others.

And it's not about the recognition given to you for having expressed your meaningful work, it's about your sense of fulfilment and service to the world for making it come alive together with yourself.

Your meaningful work that you choose to not express does not realise its potential. And neither yours, for that matter. Again, it is less important what the reason was for you making such a choice, whether you were too afraid, or too reasonable, or too busy, or too compliant, or too clever. What matters is the outcome: you are depriving your world of what could have been an essential change.

Whatever way we choose to communicate our meaningful work, the fact is that the expression of our ideas, our feelings and essentially our personality contained in our meaningful work must – metaphorically speaking – leave us and reach others in order to be realised. Otherwise, our work remains on the level of a thought, the level of an unspoken opinion, unfulfilled together with its owner.

What it means to express your meaningful work if you are a writer, a painter, a musician, an artist of any kind, may seem very clear. However, if we understand an artist to be a creator, then we all are artists, we all are creators, we all are innovators. And if you are ready to understand the material for creation in a more figurative way, you'll notice that you can create an expression from your own feelings, your own beliefs, opinions, desires, from your courage and your conviction. From connections to others, from the world's pains, from the world's joys, from your team's disengagement, from your colleagues' sense of empowerment. From whatever matters to you because it speaks directly to your meaningful work.

And so, for instance, as a creator in the down-to-earth corporate world, you can actually express your meaningful work in many ways beyond your strictly defined role description. You'll get to know these ways by staying dedicated to your passion, your integrity and your boldness.

In touch with his passion

"This leader you speak about, the person that made this huge impact on you, how would you describe him? What is it that he was or did that made such an impact on you?" As I asked him these questions, I could detect a spark in his eyes. I bet that in that very moment he was able to clearly visualise that man who had such an influence on him, clearly a different one than he was normally used to in his working environment.

He was a newly appointed director sent to coaching in order to get clarity on what really fulfils him in his new role. His coaching sponsor was a very empowered and experienced leader, and knowing the nature of their strict corporate world he believed fulfilment was what was going to help him find the right balance. The balance this sponsor had in mind was the one between my client's two realities: what makes him feel alive and what stands a pretty real chance of treading on his values in his future role.

"Umm, he was..." He paused to find the right words. "He was a human being first, and a manager second. Yes, that's who he was." He nodded as if feeling the impact of that humanity right there as he was recalling him.

"Oh wow, sounds very important. What did that mean to you?"

He answered this question right away, no umming or thinking twice. The answer was instilled deep in him: "I remember looking at him and thinking: this is the sort of leader I want to become. In all his professionalism, he never placed a human being second. He always had time to listen, patience to find the right words, enthusiasm to guide and mentor, and courage to speak about things no one really dared to." There he stopped as if digging deeper into his memories, before he continued: "And he found time to start so many important initiatives, those that changed the way we did things, and eventually that changed the way we felt in that workplace. Those that changed the level of our trust in him, and in ourselves and in the work that we were doing."

"Where do you see yourself in this man?" I asked and he immediately shouted back: "Oh I don't know, I'm not... I mean, I'd love to..." He stopped, lost in his thoughts.

"He was clearly a man who knew what mattered to him," I said.

"He was for sure."

"And it sounds as though what mattered to him, matters to you as well. Am I hearing that right?" I asked, attempting to double-check my observations.

"Oh, absolutely. You see, I never want to become the sort of a leader that stops appreciating the connection first. The one that stops caring about people. I don't want to be present in that kind of a workplace every day. Now, don't get me wrong, I'm not undermining the importance of a result; it's what brought me here and it is what matters to me as well. What I'm talking about is the balance between delivering and caring. Result and connection. Achieving and developing. Growing."

"So, if you could be mentored by this man, your role-model, right now, what would you hear him say to you? Let's say he tells you something like this: You need to act on what matters to you and here's how you start...", at which point I stopped and asked him to continue.

And he did. He sounded as if he knew exactly what the expression of his meaningful work was, while it beautifully unfolded in front of us both in that very moment. And so, we both heard loud and clear what his "to do" was and how he'd bring it into his workplace, which conversations he'd open, which ideas he'd share, which initiatives he'd push forward. As he spoke about it, excited and breathless, he felt alive.

Ronald Heifetz defined leadership as an activity, a mobilisation of the resources of people or organisations to make progress on whatever difficult issues they may be facing.[83] Bob Anderson and Bill Adams, in their leadership books, define leadership as the deployment of self into circumstance to create outcomes.[84] Notice the concepts of "activity", "mobilisation", "deployment", and "create outcomes". They all indicate that what matters to us must get expressed in some way for its fulfilment.

What the expression of your meaningful work can be in your own reality is something that you need to discover. Will you express it in terms of opening up an important conversation, changing a government policy or a company practice, starting a movement, an association, a community, raising funds, starting writing or speaking about something important, or setting a new personal example for something in your family or your wider community? Whatever it is, you will know it best.

There are occasions when by expressing your meaningful work, you will mobilise many others to create what your world needs. What starts as an individual agenda in terms of being meaningful to one person turns out to be an invitation that many others respond to, sometimes even entire systems, countries, nations. The examples of such collective expressions of meaningful energies, apart from being a concrete help and support to someone or something in the moment, remain an indelible leadership legacy serving humanity.

Standing up through our meaningful work

Just a few days before the end of 2020, a little town called Petrinja, approximately 40 km away from the Croatian capital city of Zagreb, was hit by a series of earthquakes. What started as a 5.5 Richter scale earthquake was unusually, but obviously completely possibly, followed by an even stronger 6.4 one immediately the following day, leaving behind a lot of misery and little safety that will – at best – take years to restore. Aftershocks, as they call smaller subsequent earthquakes, were raging for days after the huge catastrophe that had deepened the poverty and the fear.

Out of many things that these unfortunate events brought to the surface, one of them is most certainly the absolute lack of trust in the government and their institutions to the point of anger and disgust that was impossible to hide. However, I won't go further down that road in this book. What comes to my mind in describing the entire situation is a powerful quote in the title of the article by Ryan Holiday published in the Daily Stoic. The title is: When the System Breaks Down, Leaders Stand Up.[85] And this is exactly what happened – much or not to general surprise – people in my country rose to the occasion and they did it collectively.

And so, before you knew it, there were people from all over the country as well as those living abroad who organised themselves to help. They were bringing in food, medical supplies, caravans for the living. People volunteered to go to the impacted places and cook and repair roofs, and others volunteered to host families with children in their own home on the other end of the country. Many sent financial support. Social media was burning with requests, plans, travel routes and collaboration initiatives to support those in need.

There are no words, no words whatsoever that can explain the burning energy of connection, support, gratitude and deeply loving service. Whatever I write here cannot reflect the depth of this genuine loving service towards other human beings. I can only count on you to trust me that one cannot witness that power of human love and remain untouched and unchanged in the way one makes sense of life.

I'm not going into debates about what official charity and other institutions did or did not do or ensure; I'm deliberately focusing on the people who had no obligation to act apart from themselves feeling obliged to express their meaningful work in the most tangible way in service of their world. It was happening to an extent that was beyond imagination.

I dare to know that it was well beyond the imagination of the one who started it, the one who answered their own call for meaning. Who would even care to pinpoint that person? Was it only one person, after all, who stood up as a leader first? Who cares about anything else other than the outcome it eventually created?

The paradox is that when it happens that such a face of humanity is rarely seen in action for years, it's hard to believe in it even when it shows up clearly in front of you. When what people still deep down firmly believe in is a formal authority, mostly expecting that authority to act over and over again comes so naturally even after years of disappointment.

In the above-mentioned article, the author uses Marcus Aurelius's wisdom from his book Meditations, which refers to his context at the time, while saying that a disease like the plague, "can only threaten your life" while other things like evil, selfishness, pride, hypocrisy and fear "attack our humanity". If these things attack our humanity, then the loving expression of our meaningful work has good potential to save it and create an indelible legacy, no matter how unbelievable it may seem.

Ask yourself, what kind of a leader – formal or informal – are you to deny the power and urgency of our meaningful work?

There is a limitless boldness in all of us. One that is present in any circumstances we find ourselves in, and it awaits in our meaningful work, in our own aliveness. It's our leadership work to express this aliveness.

Because the expression of our aliveness – as Heifetz[86] says – is what exercising leadership is.

The vision and the discomfort

Expressing your meaningful work and exercising your leadership is how you walk towards your vision. You need to know that where there's a vision, there will be discomforts too. That's simply because the vision stands for risk, and the discomforts stand for what every logical part of you will tend to seek protection from. The bolder your vision is, the bigger the discomforts you encounter, and the more your needs for risk-free safety are at stake. Leadership is inseparable from the vision just as the vision is inseparable from the discomfort.

Expression of your meaningful work is the attempt to make your vision a reality. Regardless of what your vision is, as a leader you should not expect that attempt to be anything less than bold, because if you are not ready to stay committed to transforming your vision into reality, despite all the obstacles that may at moments seem reasonably impossible to overcome, what are your chances of creating a legacy that matters?

The paradox is that the world has got the obvious task of creating obstacles for us as we attempt to bring out our meaningful work, as well as simultaneously having a hidden desire to see us succeed. Because if we do, we'll prove it's possible. And one thing that the world individually and collectively craves for – despite paradoxically limiting itself from reaching it – is the possibility of realising meaning.

Bold leaders take their vision seriously and the discomfort merely as an indication of the importance of their work, an ally helping them understand who they can become together with their worlds as they stay committed to their deeply meaningful vision.

Your reflection

Here are a few questions to reflect on:

1. Think of the change your world needs. What about that change depends upon your commitment to expressing your meaningful work?

2. How serious are you about your meaningful vision, and how bold in the face of the accompanying discomforts? What is well worth the commitment and the risk?

3. What else requires you to pause and reflect?

CHAPTER 12: Game Changers

THIS IS ONE of the definitions of a game changer: "An event, idea, or procedure that effects a significant shift in the current way of doing or thinking about something"[87]. That could refer to your, my, our leadership bringing change to the status quo of our world.

I believe that our world is in imperative need of such leadership. That means that it is in the imperative need of leaders who find meaning in taking the personal risk to change anything that adds meaning to their world on a larger scale and they take action to mobilise others to join them in this work. I define them as game changers.

There are three key qualities describing the most effortless essence of game changers: integrity, curiosity and boldness. They lead with courage, consciousness and conviction. They lead with full hearts and not faint hearts. Most of all, they lead out of the very fullness of their soul, with the full capacity of their desires as human beings.

As they lead, what they enthusiastically embrace is: going upstream. Because the world is more often and more importantly changed by the readiness of people to go upstream than by those who make sure they remain swimming with the current.

Regardless of the imperative need of our world, we are taught very little about how to be game changers. There is frequent discussion accompanied by training efforts on how we need to be team players. While being a team player is just as essential for the prosperity of our world, I cannot help but question if this imperative is sometimes served as a Trojan horse – a trick deceptively standing for an aligned collaboration, while genuinely trying to get us into submission and unquestionable acceptance of whatever is being served to all of us. We accept the gift so as not to challenge the harmony, which by the way could well be artificial and perhaps beneficial only to those who served it. I doubt that it's beneficial even to them in the long run.

If we were committed to our collective conscious legacy of developing more truly devoted game changers in our worlds, all our team play would flourish and reach different levels, and could even be renamed as what's essentially more empowering: collective leadership.

Our world craves game changers, those ready to bring their radical quests to re-examine the world's status quo, to repurpose leadership in the service of humanity and a more meaningful world as its home.

Next level boldness

Game changers envision a humanity that strives to be bigger than individuals' interests, fears or limitations. Their belief is that human development is a starting and an ending point of all endeavours, in whatever business, whatever institution, whatever part of our society. They are the leaders ready to transform, be transformed and serve.

Game changers bring next level boldness to their leadership because they bring next level consciousness to understanding the world. Their active concern goes to all pillars of society, whatever those pillars are that they see as important in protecting humanity. In whatever they attempt to change, they strongly stand for the development and care of human beings first, and things second.

Dedicated to bettering their worlds from that perspective, they are the initiators of all the conversations that we as humans must not leave unopen. With this concept in mind, I remember the words of one of my clients: "We're just in the business of furniture." This is what she would say when, in the face of what went deeply against her integrity, her limiting beliefs prevailed over her game-changing vision of humanity and her boldness to pursue it.

The thing is, it is never just the furniture, pipes, cables or applications. Even if we are not literally holding a human heart in our hands, we are responsible for what saves – or not – our humanity. It's always the people involved. And we, as game changers, as bold leaders, have the responsibility to radically question the status quo of everything that surrounds us and offer our leadership quest as a more human reality than what our current surrounding one may be.

Let's look at this through the lens of what's easier to hold. It is easier to believe that we are not in the business that shapes humanity. It is easier to believe that, unlike everyone impacting our world, only some pillars of society do so, making them therefore the only ones responsible. It is easier to believe that we simply have to leave some businesses, some corporate worlds because we tell ourselves that things cannot be changed there and we cannot have the impact we desire. Metaphorically speaking, it's as if we're leaving a ship that's sinking. The only thing is, it is not sinking, it is sailing further, shaping our collective waves that we have given up surfing and therefore given up both the possibility and the responsibility of impacting potential change.

Some may find this confronting depending perhaps on the experience they had in their corporate world. But here's what I'm convinced of: game changers do not leave. They lead. Even when they get kicked out of the game, or literally out of their office for that matter. And to lead – in their vocabulary – is to first question everything and then do the work to help transform whatever calls for transformation. Together.

So, taking this to a more granular level: How is it that the game changers do their work? I'll answer this question by starting from what they **have**, what they **create** and finally how they **show up** in their work.

Game changers always **have** the ***Initiative***. That means they first have an idea of what could bring a significant shift in the current way of doing or thinking about something. Their environment inspires them with the idea: their workplace or any other part of their society that impacts the quality of their life and the life of their world. There is a huge sense of accountability involved here. Secondly, they are ready to bring this idea to life; they are ready to invest their different resources to make the change happen, which is the first step from an idea to an initiative. In the realm of ***Universe***, you learnt about the difference between a leader having an opinion and having a voice. Notice how game changers bring their leadership to take their concern to the next level – having a voice becomes more concrete as it transforms into an actual initiative for change.

Game changers' initiatives are larger than themselves as individuals, which often means that they are risky, but also that they have the potential to bring a significant shift. Their initiatives, as said before, often stand for the upstream swim. Game changers also know that anything that's larger than us is created together. And so, the first thing they do, having the initiative, is to **create** a ***Circle***: gather and connect with people ready to join them in their ideas.

Here comes a crucial distinction: even if the Initiative is initially created by a game changer, it continues to be co-created by the Circle. Whatever has the potential to significantly shift the status quo must involve accountable co-leaders rather than a group of tacit followers. This can be one of the most delicate steps in the process that often relies on nothing but our ability to lead with the radical connection approach in the realm of ***Other***, while learning of the importance of trust and calling forth everyone involved, including ourselves.

In the Circle, no one is a spectator. Everyone is a leader and everyone activates leadership in themselves and others. You've noticed by now that it is a drastically different space, reserved for other behaviours than the ones our brain is normally wired for: complaining, blaming, complying, controlling and proving right. And yet it's possible, if you boldly step into it. Game changers know that that too is a part of changing the game.

As they co-lead the Initiative within the Circle, game changers **show up** with ***Integrity, Curiosity and Boldness***. Much has been said about these characteristics throughout this book. In this particular place, these elements act as allies to the game changers in their potentially vulnerable moments, such as those in which their initiatives grow bigger than their initial idea or perhaps take different directions in the ever-changing reality.

Rather than being attached to their originally constructed initiative, game changers stay in a learning mode, allowing for creative conflict as a tool for pressure testing the idea. That is how they stay in the right place of contributing to the purpose of the idea and the circle gathered to make it reality. In the process of co-leading their Initiative, integrity helps game changers to stay true to what they know at their core: curiosity to be open to what they can still learn, and boldness to hold both of these perspectives if they – as they usually do – happen to be in conflict.

Game changers are the champions in sensing and answering the urge for a bold action that can create much needed change always and in all places. Notice the fact that they can be outspoken extroverts as much as reflective introverts. It's not about the way they present themselves. It's about the way they are ready to risk for what they believe in, letting go of their comfort to ensure their contribution.

Game changers always dare to know what is calling for their leadership, even more so in the midst of great discomfort.

I believe it is the daring – and not the knowing – that enables us to change any game. What's important is that we stay committed and keep trying, even in the moments when what we're left with is no guarantee, but only our best assumption of the future change and the possibility of succeeding with it.

Our future world deserves game changers now. Creative minds ready to connect the dots and willing to embrace the invitation for change that will make us more and not less human. They may do it through the inquisitiveness of their intellect, their intuition or simply their bold heart, or very likely through all of those sources. They are simply bold souls who dare to listen and answer their world's needs with the best of their intentions.

Call to bold action now

If you have understood the discussion so far about game changers as a call to your own bold action, I've made my point. If you haven't, I'm making my invitation to you right now.

Start. Now.

So, what am I actually inviting you to do, trusting that you will accept and then pass this invitation on to others?

I'm inviting you to have your mind, heart and gut awakened to what your corner of the world looks like and how it operates. What's happening in the pillars of society that your world consists of: in the business world, education system, politics, justice, health system? What concerns you in terms of how these pillars contribute to the current and future image of your world? I know you do have an opinion. You know that having an opinion is not enough. And so, what will you do?

Because what game changers do, is they take their opinion to further steps. What's the point of not agreeing with the direction in which we swim, if we still continue to go with the current? The potential of such an attitude is nothing but the creation of a complaining and blaming culture, rather than the culture of bold leadership.

The truth is that we all have something to complain about – something that we experience in our organisations and our institutions that goes against our integrity-based vision. In the context of game changers, this is simply how we look at it: the urge to complain is the urge for change. Bring your leadership instead to support the emerging change, the reality in the making.

You'll hear a lot that visionary leaders have a dream, a vision, even a quest. Game changers also clearly know they have work to do. In fact, they look for it. Let's be specific. They find their work to do as they watch the education system their children are being raised by. They find their work to do as they witness the reliability and the credibility of their justice system or the service of their political system. They find their work to do as they observe their business environment and the way that it is clearly shaping the rest of the world.

Not everything is our work and we do not need to change the entire world. But it is essential we understand that something is our work and that every work has its start somewhere, even in a circle as small as a parent-teacher meeting. The actual measurement, in the end, is always the impact. So, where do you start creating your game changing impact, today?

As they undertake their work, the game changers create impact that can change the direction in which their worlds go no matter where they start from. The requirement is to willingly hold the discomfort of the bigger, bolder game they are playing. To step into the arena committed to their vision at the cost of their safety.

I cannot say what your exact arena is, because none of us can say what other people's arena is. But we can all clearly sense what our own arena is. And we cannot invite others into it, until we have first stepped into it ourselves.

I hope that by now you have no doubts that this is not about the game changers' role or ambition to save the world as heroes. It's about their sense of accountability to invite the world to save itself by role-modelling boldness, often role-modelling what it means to stand up for the common good when their personal comfort is at stake.

Game changers are not hero fighters. They are conscious and intentional servant warriors. The focus of their initiatives is to make the world become more human-like, more connecting, more meaningful and more sustainable. Rather than aiming high, game changers aim deep. That often means that they start from going deeply into the learning process of what their own leadership is, and what the one is that their world needs. Rather than inspiring ambition, they inspire bold, courageous, ethical and compassionate living and leading. A caring action with unshakeable devotion to what matters most from the place as deep as the human soul.

Perhaps you'll add to the perspectives of what game changers are. Please do and let me say clearly what they are not. Game changers are not spectators. Collective leadership legacy, or any for that matter, cannot be created by spectators. From whichever angle we approach leadership, we see all the different concepts and theories having one thing in common: they stand for an invitation to natural human boldness, genuine human greatness, the potential of human bigness. Not for the reason of individual glorification, but for the reason of us as leaders being active contributors to the meaningfulness of this world.

And so, instead of being a timid soul – as Theodore Roosevelt says in his most famous speech – "who neither know victory, nor defeat", be a bold one "who knows great enthusiasms, the great devotions; who spends himself in a worthy cause".

Awaken your great enthusiasm, your great devotions, find your worthy cause, discover your meaningful work and leave a legacy, a conscious imprint in this world that, regardless of its scale and nature, does take part in a process of an emerging change – the process lasting in the world for as long as the world itself.

You're not sure where to start from? Consider this perspective and the answer will appear: you owe it to yourself and your world to resolve any inner dilemma that prevents the expression of your boldness in service of your legacy. You are accountable for not refusing the gift of your game changing leadership potential in exchange for – only seemingly – safe and comfortable bystander's shoes.

Whether you are ready to accept this perspective or not quite yet, the truth may well lie in the title of the beautifully deep David Whyte poem: "Everything Is Waiting for You".[88] Following the inspiration of this title, let us also look for the hard truth in what is a quote often attributed to Buddha: "The trouble is, you think you have time."

We collectively think we have time.

And in fact, the awareness of the lack of time is our best ally in resolving our most important dilemmas around how to act. Steve Jobs said it much better than me: "Remembering that I'll be dead soon is the most important tool I've ever encountered to help me make the big choices in life. Remembering that you are going to die is the best way I know to avoid the trap of thinking you have something to lose. You are already naked."

How you wish to play with the fact of your nakedness in the game of life and leadership, what coat you wish to wear and how soon within the limited time framework, is really just a matter of your own choice. But it's one choice that will eventually impact all of us.

Your reflection

Here are a few questions to reflect on:

1. What's your arena? Have you stepped in?

2. Even though time is a limited concept, the world will always be patiently waiting for you to step in. The question is – what are you waiting for?

3. What else requires you to pause and reflect?

Before proceeding to the Epilogue, here's an invitation for you:

Great leaders are game changers.

Visit www.boldleadership-culture.com and schedule a strategy call with me to discuss how to bring the **SOUL framework** to your personal and organisational leadership either face-to-face or through my online programmes.

EPILOGUE

ALMOST EVERY STORY that I hear from leaders in the coaching and leadership development space reveals the same pattern they struggle with: the tension[89] between what makes them feel safe and what makes them feel alive.

As they speak, I hear them continuously dance on the string between these two polarities: there is something they want so much and there's a fear that goes with it. When I teach them about the concept that sees leadership as a game in which one either plays to win or plays to not lose[90], some openly state: "I'd rather not lose than win. I can't explain, but somehow it gives me a better feeling, it's more important. I guess I don't really care about winning." In this context, winning refers to whatever it is that they want and that lives on the other side of their fear.

Here's how I see it: this choice they say they'd rather have gives them a feeling of comfort; that's what this instant better feeling is. And it is nothing more than that: an instant, a moment, a glimpse of always really unreachable safety. And to believe our own illusion, we say we don't really care about what we may have won. A great way to start dying before time.

Another way to look at this tension is through our ego-minds limiting the potential of our souls.[91] When the fear-based beliefs of our ego-mind have a final say in our decision-making process, which means that they are pushing us to choose safety over our own growth, over our next level Self, we are in fact limiting the potential of our soul, the Self that we could become.

The term I use in this book is a leadership dilemma between vision and comfort. In fact, I've presented it through the bold leaders' capacity to hold both vision and discomfort at the same time.

It means that we all have a vision, a desire, a longing for something that really matters, but not all of us dare to lead that vision because it is hard to stay with the discomfort. We would like to eliminate it even at the expense of our vision, not step into the bigger version of ourselves, even if that means remaining smaller than what we could have become. In fact, this is the essence of many, if not all, the stories leaders bring to their coaching and development process, at least with me.

This dilemma happens a million times a day. The magnitude of the question or the stake may be different, but the dilemma is always there.

It is present every time we take a decision about speaking up, confronting someone, sharing something, deciding on any action, and any approach. It's always there. And resolving it in service of our vision always comes at the cost of our comfort.

Now that we've normalised this dilemma as a common struggle for every leader, every human being, all of us, we also need to speak the hard-loving truth and say that no one can face it for us. For any of us.

It's neither going to disappear, and nor is someone else going to solve it to our comfort. There is no solution to this dilemma other than we who need to dare to know what's more important for us. Out of the two things that matter, we resolve it by choosing the one that matters more and with the awareness that this choice will define our leadership.

And here's what is really important about this individual dilemma: it will very much define our collective leadership as well. Because the world in which everyone chooses to play small, or play to not lose, can hardly show itself as being great in the sense of alive and empowered.

This means great in the sense of any quality that best serves humanity and its development. We are all at the receiving end of what our world provides, so if we don't like what we experience we may wish to revisit our inner dilemma more often.

We may wish to revisit it right now. We may need to remind ourselves that we as leaders eventually add up either to the greatness or to the smallness of our world.

This dilemma eventually becomes a conversation about what leadership identity we choose to adopt. As leaders I believe we have a choice of two: either we adopt the identity of a fighter or the identity of a warrior.

With the fighter identity, we fight for comfort as our human need, against any pain or loss or threat; we fight to restore our power to keep what we have, what we know and what makes us safe as such.

There's a lot of righteousness involved in the identity of a fighter, and even though not necessarily immediately visible, there's a lot of victim mentality as well. It's a path to a win-lose game, the mindset of "It's happening to me but I will survive". Fighter identity is the one that keeps you in life, but rather than making you feel alive it makes you exhausted by struggle.

There's nothing wrong with this attitude. It's human to say the least. Still, as much as this identity may seem bold, its boldness will not take us to the next level, to reinvent our own and our joint leadership. Because the boldness that has the potential to do that requires us to access our soul to search for some important meaning to make our leadership game bigger.

To be bold takes your soul, and leaders with the fighter identity do not explore their soul because they don't have the time; they've got a fight to lead instead to re-establish their sense of safety.

Reinventing bold leadership takes warriors. Leaders that will stand up not for comfort, but to realise their vision that brings aliveness to them and their world despite the accompanying presence of personal discomfort.

Some of my clients, colleagues and friends are true warriors. I recognise them by their courage, their capacity to dare, their conscious sense of self and their sense of responsibility and accountability for their world.

Most of all I recognise them by their conviction that they are doing the right thing, that they are risking for the right cause, for the right vision, the right sense of *why* even if it feels unbearably uncomfortable at times. Their conviction is contagious.

Leaders with the warrior identity lead with the next level of their courage, their consciousness and their conviction.

As they do so, they are still faced with a dilemma. But what they are not faced with is whether the risk of choosing their vision over their comfort makes sense in the overall context of their leadership service.

Bold warrior leaders are not confused as to whether they are actually leading or merely surviving. Let me for a moment go back to my own experience described in the Prologue of this book. The event that happened and that has triggered a number of other related situations to date, all of which have been most uncomfortable for me, is not the conversation about surviving. Taking a narrow-minded view, you could say that I did not survive that very day. It was the end of my leadership.

That, in fact, could not be further from the truth. Rather than being an opportunity to survive the end of something, our most uncomfortable experiences are the edges we are faced with. Not the end – the edge, instead. Crossing it is not the opportunity to survive, but to create a bigger, bolder version of self. The bigger the edge, the bolder your next level self.

When you step boldly into that discomfort, life offers most interesting stories. For instance, I met my husband within the team that was helping me with the legal side of my experience. Today, we have a super bright and super bold little warrior son that has brought a different dimension to both of our lives. I've changed my career which allows me to honour my deepest values of travel, cultural diversity and learning. People that I'm meeting, learning from and working with in different parts of the world have immeasurably enriched my life. I've reopened some of my long-abandoned dreams of what I really wanted to create.

In fact, it has all brought a different level of maturity into my life: different roles, different learnings, different risks and different ways to approach them.

The taste of my life a decade ago is incomparable with how my life tastes now in all its current experiences and future dreams. Some elements of my current life are to a great extent more uncomfortable, just as all its elements are to a great extent more meaningful. I'm simply choosing fulfilment over comfort, convinced that that's what makes life truly worth living.

In practical language, what really happened is that my decision-making pattern has radically changed. I am faced with ever-appearing edges and ever-present dilemmas every day and I stay conscious to whether I shrink or expand as a result of my choices.

When we shrink or we expand endless times a day, making ourself and our world smaller or greater, we all do it by choice to avoid or not the risk of it. Avoiding risk, eventually, is avoiding the joy of life and our birthright to be boldly free.

By now you must have learnt about my firm belief: conversations design our life, our work, our world, our whole reality. The more uncomfortable they are, the more they are needed.

The conversation around how bold our personal leadership is, is not the most comfortable one for any of us. It's a daring one and the one that is very much needed.

Therefore, I'd like to invite you to reach out to me to deepen this daring conversation.

Let's discuss how we can keep reinventing what bold really is by taking our collective leadership from "survive" to "alive" as we bring this work to you and your organisation. As a result, we'll create a more meaningful world for all of us.

If this book has made an impact on you, please stay in touch.

These are the ways to communicate with me directly:

- via my personal email zana@boldleadership-culture.com
- via my LinkedIn profile www.linkedin.com/in/zanagoicpetricevic

I'll be happy to hear from you.

You can also visit my site www.boldleadership-culture.com to subscribe for more thought leadership content and resources.

And whatever you do, for the sake of our world, please stay bold.

Jumpstart your bold leadership

Self

1. Our leadership work that makes us feel alive and serves the larger context of our world is risky. The soul work in our development helps us find meaning to this risk.

2. Leadership is not just about what we do in the workplace. It is about who we are and how we make sense of the world.

3. Bold leaders have a hunger for learning in all circumstances, because they have an insatiable hunger for meaning.

4. There is something most bold in our choice to accept the practice of learning as a way of living and leading in all circumstances: confronting one's current self in the service of creating the next level self.

5. When evolving leadership consciousness becomes a collective hunger, the world will stop starving for prosperity.

6. The path to this higher level of consciousness goes through the painful depths of your comfort zones.

7. Nothing reduces the possibility of innovation more than a conservative fixed know-it-all-so-I-don't-need-it attitude. There is not one field where you could not always learn more, including yourself. There is nothing to which you could not go deeper, if you dared.

8. Leadership development begins by meeting our own purpose. Meeting our own purpose is a disciplined practice of listening to what our soul desires, to what truly matters to us when liberated from the protective shackles of our ego, from the fear. It eventually means honouring our own responsibility to express ourselves from the very core of our being in doing our work in the world.

9. We understand the world through our own stories, which are in fact assumptions that we call truths.

10. To understand our reality, we need to understand our illusions. We, as leaders, are invited to constantly disrupt them.

11. The true art of self-disruption is to involve the many intelligences we possess.

12. We disrupt ourselves; we explore ourselves; we heal ourselves, just to be able to meet our world with our new bigger, bolder story.

13. Once we start eagerly owning our new story, we start adding new value to our world.

14. We cannot hold two Self versions. We can shrink into the old one or we can expand within the new one. Our impact will eventually tell.

Other

15. Leadership as radical connection means that we do not feel immediately invited to look for whether we can trust other people or not, but we

instead consciously make ourselves wired to look for the wisdom in other people, which will automatically make us both wiser.

16. Leadership lives in a hard-loving truth. Much of leadership is opening up the conversations that we know are needed and that feel most uncomfortable.

17. Leading the other changes us both. We are ready to undoubtedly believe in each other's potential.

18. What I see in you is what I've got in me.

19. Connection is not an illusion. Separateness is.

20. Connection leads to inspiration and empowerment. It leads to people you lead feeling accountable for each other's good, for the common good, the good of the whole.

21. The good news is that trust is a choice. When our leadership matures, we learn that trust is a matter of personal decision.

22. Integrity is the sign of me trusting my own wholeness.

23. Leading others from the place of their approval of you suffocates your boldness.

24. Intimacy is much more about the truth than anything else. It is as much about the ability to say as it is about the ability to hear.

25. Feedback is much more about our readiness for intimacy than our possession of good communication skills.

26. Intimacy is deepening the relationship. Distance is deepening the pain.

27. Without intimacy leadership is transactional rather than relational. All head and no heart.

28. Real leadership is vulnerable, showing the real side of our humanness.

29. Controlling happens in the absence of trust.

30. When it comes to caring connection, time is an excuse. When leaders' hearts are sensitive to their people's stories, their clocks adjust.

31. The less tough conversations there are, the less safety there is in the workplace. Hard-loving truth in all its discomfort is in fact a way of increasing safety among those leading and being led.

32. See the faces of the people you lead. Meet their eyes. What is it that you are longing for them?

Universe

33. Leadership is not a matter of power. It's a matter of concern.

34. We willingly embrace the illusion of powerlessness because the short-term personal safety feels so much more reasonable than what we know may be collectively needed in the long run.

35. Bold leaders speak up in the culture of silence even when it's most risky.

36. Bold leaders see confrontation as a path to creativity and meaningful work through radically open conversations.

37. For their leadership to come to life by using their voice, bold leaders need to listen first.

38. The land of the unspoken is built by all of us keeping quiet, and what's not being said gradually becomes heard even louder.

39. When people can't speak or at least they assume they can't, they lose meaning.

40. If bold leaders have any sixth sense, it is the sense of speech.

41. Leadership is an intentional sport that cannot be played well unconsciously.

42. Bold leaders create from the unspoken. They believe that all voices matter.

43. Unfolding the unspoken initiates the change.

44. Bolder conversations are never about who's right and who's wrong but about what is and what's next for whoever is engaging in them.

45. Bold leaders activate leadership in everyone.

46. Bold leaders bring their integrity to work to create safety in the workplace so that these conversations can actually happen.

47. Bold leaders are aware of the distinction between having advice and having a voice.

48. The opportunities for us to act as leaders are everywhere. The positions of formal authority are scarce compared to the number of these opportunities.

49. We lead boldly by welcoming the daring enquiry rather than the safe instructions. Bold leadership is defined by the questions that we dare to ask and stay with, and not by our addiction to the right answers.

Legacy

50. It is the daring – and not necessarily the knowing – that enables us to change any game.

51. Every person leaves a legacy.

52. Our work, the one we are here to do, has an inevitable potential to outlast our life. You can call it a purpose. You'll recognise it by the way it pulls you to itself, grabs the attention of your mind and gets hold of your heart centred in the middle of your soul.

53. Discovering your meaningful work starts with the awareness of what your soul desires. Nurturing those desires means feeding love to our dreams as opposed to suppressing the hunger of our insatiable fears.

54. The change that makes the world more human is always worth the risk.

55. Bold leaders come alive through the meaningful work they are here to do for their worlds.

56. Meaningful work leads to purposeful achievements.

57. Love, not drive, is in the centre of our passion.

58. Denying your passion that would serve your world is to deny your integrity.

59. Meaningful work is our expression of the deepest love of our soul that we have the courage to keep choosing in service of our world.

60. There is no leadership legacy without expression. Keeping your meaningful work for yourself is denying the contribution to others.

61. Where there's a vision, there will be discomforts too. Leadership is inseparable from the vision just as the vision is inseparable from the discomfort.

62. Bold leaders take their vision seriously and the discomfort merely as an indication of the importance of their work.

63. As they lead, game changers enthusiastically embrace going upstream. Because the world is more often and more importantly changed by the

readiness of people to go upstream than by those who make sure they remain swimming with the current.

64. Game changers bring the next level boldness to their leadership because they bring next level consciousness to understanding the world.

65. Leaders struggle with the tension between what makes them feel safe and what makes them feel alive, the dilemma between vision and comfort.

66. Leaders add up either to the greatness or to the smallness of their world.

67. Leaders can adopt the identity of a fighter or the identity of a warrior.

68. With the fighter identity, leaders fight to restore their power to keep what they have, and what makes them safe as such.

69. Leaders with the warrior identity bring their three inner allies to their bold leadership: their courage, their consciousness, their conviction.

Appendix

The Leadership Circle Profile™ (*LCP*) and Collective Leadership Assessment™ (*CLA*)

Introducing the breakthrough 360° profile that connects patterns of action with habits of thought: **Leadership Circle Profile™ *(LCP)***

Leadership Circle Profile™ is a true breakthrough among 360-degree assessments. It is the first to connect a well-researched battery of competencies with the underlying motivations and habits of thought. It reveals the relationship between patterns of action and the internal assumptions that drive behaviour.

LCP goes to the source of behaviour to get greater leverage on change. Furthermore, unlike most leadership 360-degree assessments, which take hours to interpret, *LCP* integrates all this information in a way that brings the key issues to the surface instantly. The data in *LCP* reveals itself in seconds. At a glance, the whole gestalt is accessible. It immediately gets your leader in touch with what is working, what is not, and why!

In most organisations, this treasure trove of information remains buried. *LCP* makes it easily accessible while it creates a foundation on which change can occur at a deeper level and a sustainable pace.

Leadership Circle Profile Benefits:

- More Revealing – the Leadership Circle Profile (LCP) is the only leadership 360 assessment that *connects patterns of behaviour* with *habits of thought.*
- More Advanced – it instantly reveals key opportunities for your leader's development without reams of documentation.
- More than just an assessment – The rich theoretical underpinnings of LCP provide a pathway to transformation. No other assessment of this type offers this.
- More Efficient – It allows the coach to start at a breakthrough point with a leader rather than spend months trying to reach one.
- More Dynamic – HR professionals, leaders, and seasoned consultants/coaches, consistently report that LCP facilitates authentic, breakthrough results.
- Widely Accepted – LCP is truly world class and used by a vast number of leading local, national, and international organisations and government agencies.

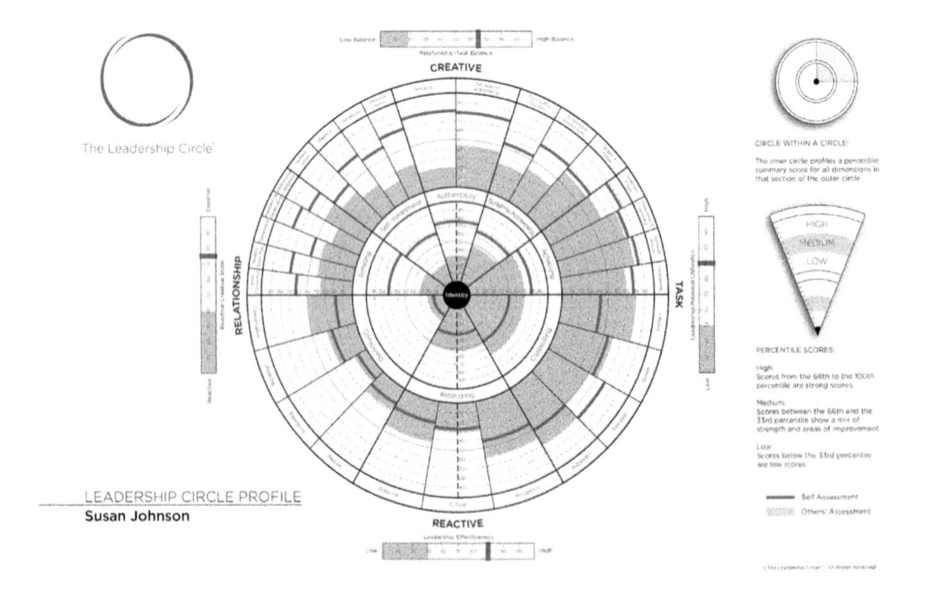

Get a thorough and valid assessment of your organisation's collective leadership effectiveness: **Collective Leadership Assessment™ *(CLA)***

Collective Leadership Assessment™ delivers a powerful "litmus" test of your collective leadership effectiveness. Used for your entire organisation, or just a leadership team, the Collective Leadership Assessment reveals valuable data: It tells you how your people view their current leadership culture, and compares that reality to the optimal culture they desire. The "gap" between data on the current state and the desired outcome instantly reveals key opportunities for collective leadership development. Furthermore, the Collective Leadership Assessment measures how your collective leadership effectiveness compares to that of other organisations.

Collective Leadership Assessment provides an affordable, web based and user-friendly insight into your culture as influenced by collective leadership. Results are downloadable for immediate access. The CLA provides you the ability to choose whether you want to assess organisation collective leadership, business unit collective leadership or individual team collective leadership.

The Collective Leadership Assessment will:

- Establish a compelling rationale for change.
- Focus leadership development efforts.
- Delineate cultural challenges associated with acquisitions, mergers and restructuring plans.
- Correlate leadership to productivity, profits, turnover and other bottom line metrics.

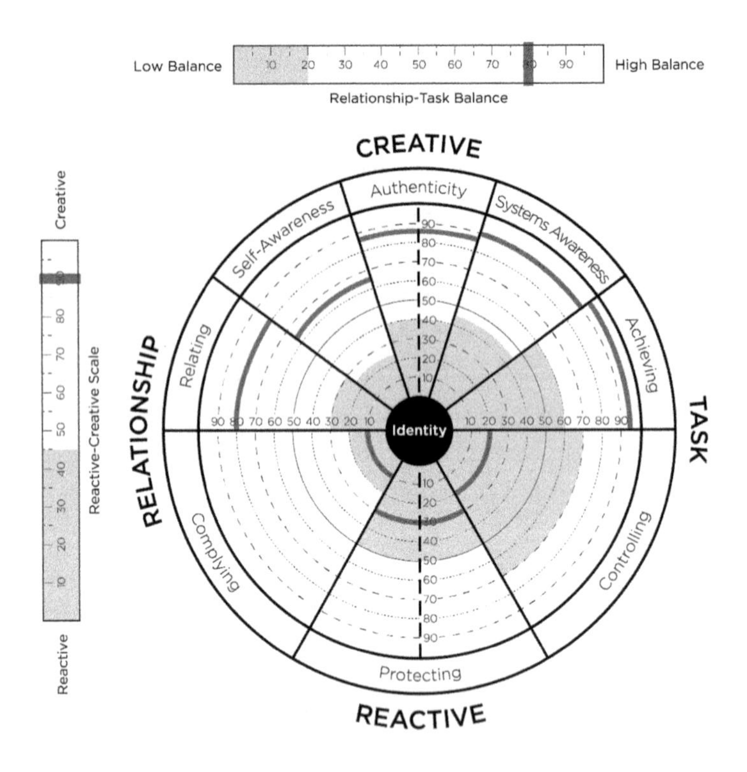

Schedule a strategy call with me to bring these benefits to you and your organisation

Besides being a member of the Leadership Circle Community®, I am certified in Leadership Circle Profile™, and Collective Leadership Assessment™ and therefore authorised to bring these tools into my leadership development coaching and consulting business to help you increase your individual leadership effectiveness and the leadership effectiveness of your entire organisation.

Schedule a strategy call with me to discuss how we can apply Leadership Circle Profile™, and Collective Leadership Assessment™ and bring their benefits to you and your organisation.

Prior to the call, I invite you to go to https://self-assessment.theleadershipcircle.com to do the free LCP self-assessment, so that we can have a real conversation around your self-assessment results and better understand the ways we can apply this leadership development approach within your organisation.

Visit www@boldleadership-culture.com or email me at zana@boldleadership-culture.com to schedule our conversation.

Notes

1. Brené Brown, 2018, Courage Over Comfort: Rumbling with Shame, Accountability, and Failure at Work, https://brenebrown.com/blog/2018/03/13/courage-comfort-rumbling-shame-accountability-failure-work/#close-popup
2. Leadership Circle Profile™ is created and owned by The Leadership Circle®.
3. Robert Kegan and Lisa Laskow Lahey, 2016, *An Everyone Culture: Becoming a Deliberately Developmental Organization*, Harvard Business School Publishing, p.26.
4. Co-Active Training Institute
5. Leadership Circle Profile™, Collective Leadership Assessment™, and Universal Model of Leadership™, are created and owned by The Leadership Circle®.
6. The certification programme as found at https://crrglobal.com
7. Peter Block, 2003, *The Answer to How is Yes*, Berrett-Koehler Publishers, Inc, p.7.
8. Werner Erhard, https://wernererhardquotes.wordpress.com/2010/01/22/responsibility-begins-with-the-willingness-to-take-the-stand-that-one-is-cause-in-the-matter-of-one's-life-it-is-a-declaration-not-an-assertion-that-is-it-is-a-context-from-which-one-choos/
9. Gabrielle Roth, *Sweat Your Prayers: The Five Rhythms of the Soul: Movement as Spiritual Practice*, 1998, Tarcher/Putnam. Taken from the Croatian version, 2009, *Isplesi svoje molitve, Pokret kao duhovna praksa*, Planetopija, p.199.

10. “Daring to know” is a term often used in leadership development. It refers to our decision to trust an inner knowing that something is the right thing to do.
11. Leadership Circle Profile™, Collective Leadership Assessment™, and Universal Model of Leadership™, are created and owned by The Leadership Circle®.
12. The validity study of this tool was successfully conducted by the Institute for Psychological Research and Application (IPRA) within the Industrial Organizational Psychology Department at Bowling Green State University in Bowling Green, Ohio, USA.
13. Leadership Circle Profile™, Collective Leadership Assessment™, and Universal Model of Leadership™ are created and owned by The Leadership Circle®.
14. Robert Kegan, Lisa Laskow Lahey, 2009, *Immunity to Change: How to Overcome it and Unlock Potential in Yourself and Your Organization*, Harvard Business Press, p.29.
15. Ronald A. Heifetz, Marty Linsky and Alexander Grashow, 2009, *The Practice of Adaptive Leadership*, Harvard Business Review Press, Kindle Edition, location 456.
16. The Co-Active Coaching Model is based on four cornerstones that coaches follow when they use this model. One of them says: People are naturally creative, resourceful and whole, https://coactive.com/about/what-is-coactive/
17. Anderson and Adams, the creators of the Universal Model of Leadership, speak about the two games of leadership in their book *Mastering Leadership* (2016, p.29).
18. Anderson, Adams, 2016, *Mastering Leadership: An Integrated Framework for Breakthrough Performance and Extraordinary Business Results*, Wiley, p.30.
19. Eric Hoffer, https://www.goodreads.com/quotes/146081-in-a-time-of-drastic-change-it-is-the-learners
20. “At the edge we may feel uncomfortable, events seem to be against us, and they may frighten or even, shock us” (Mindell, 2000, *Quantum Mind: The edge between physics and psychology*, Lao Tse Press, p. 66, quoted in Gronda, Hellene, 2013, https://www.processwork.org/files/Hellene%20Gronda%20Final%20Project.pdf, p.27).

21. Leadership Circle Profile™ and the Universal Model of Leadership™ are created and owned by The Leadership Circle®. Visit the Appendix of this book to learn more.
22. Profile Interpretation Manual, The Leadership Circle®, Version TLC 10.1, p.29.
23. Profile Interpretation Manual, The Leadership Circle®, Version TLC 10.1, p.23.
24. Personal Learner is the sub-competency of the Self Awareness dimension that has a 0.50 correlation to the Business Performance Index. The correlation between Business Performance and Leadership Effectiveness is 0.61. Correlation is a measurement of a statistical relationship between two variables.
25. In Organisation and Relationship Systems Coaching, Metaskill™ is used as an attitude, stance, philosophy or "come from place" that the coach stands in when coaching. The Relationship Systems Coach learns to create intentional emotional fields that promote a certain mood to positively impact the coaching. Metaskills have been created by Amy Mindell to describe the feeling attitudes that strongly affect our work and lives. To find out more, consult Amy and Arnold Mindell's work in the field of Process-oriented Psychology, also called Processwork: Amy Mindell, *Metaskills: The Spiritual Art of Therapy*, Lao Tse Press. See also Anne Rød, Marita Fridjhon, *Creating Intelligent Teams: Leading with Relationship Systems Intelligence*, KR Publishing.
26. Amanda Gorman, https://edition.cnn.com/2021/01/20/politics/amanda-gorman-inaugural-poem-transcript/index.html
27. Robert J. Anderson, William A. Adams, 2016, *Mastering Leadership: An Integrated Framework for Breakthrough Performance and Extraordinary Business Results*, Wiley, p.245.
28. "Dare" film, https://www.youtube.com/watch?v=sb2YOg_dkQM
29. SQ refers to spiritual intelligence. For more information, see Danah Zohar and Ian Marshall's book, 2012, *Spiritual Intelligence*, Bloomsbury Publishing, Kindle Edition, location 58.
30. Leadership Circle Profile™ is created and owned by The Leadership Circle®.
31. Alan Seale, https://transformationalpresence.org/alan-seale-blog/head-heart-gut-which-one-is-your-inner-leader/

32. Amanda Blake, 2019, *Your Body is Your Brain: Leverage Your Somatic Intelligence to Find Purpose, Build Resilience, Deepen Relationships and Lead More Powerfully*, Trokay Press.
33. ORSC/RSI, https://crrglobal.com/about/rsi/
34. Danah Zohar, 2012, *Spiritual Intelligence*, Bloomsbury Publishing, Kindle Edition, location 58.
35. Rick Tamlyn, 2013, *Play Your Bigger Game: 9 Minutes To Learn, A Lifetime To Live*, Hay House, Inc., p.xiv.
36. Lisa Laskow Lahey and Robert Kegan, 2009, *Immunity to Change: How to Overcome It and Unlock the Potential in Yourself and Your Organization*, Harvard Business School Publishing Corporation.
37. The Co-Active Leadership programme teaches about certain types of leaders based on their impact. This description refers to "a Danger type".
38. Leadership Circle Profile™ is created and owned by The Leadership Circle®.
39. Profile Interpretation Manual, The Leadership Circle®, Version TLC 10.1, p.38.
40. Betty Sue Flowers, C. Otto Scharmer, Joseph Jaworski, Peter M. Senge, 2005, *Presence: Exploring Profound Change in People, Organizations and Society*, Nicholas Brealey Publishing, Kindle Edition, location 3200.
41. Leadership Circle Profile™ and Collective Leadership Assessment™ are created and owned by The Leadership Circle®.
42. Marianne Williamson, https://marianne.com
43. Leadership Circle Profile™ is created and owned by The Leadership Circle®.
44. Profile Interpretation Manual, The Leadership Circle®, Version TLC 10.1, p.11.
45. Karen Kimsey-House, Henry Kimsey-House, 2015, *Co-Active Leadership: Five Ways to Lead*, Berrett-Koehler Publishers, p.15.
46. Thich Nhat Hanh, https://awakeningvisions.com/blogs/blog/thich-nhat-hanh-quotes
47. Rumi, https://www.goodreads.com/quotes/848553-you-are-not-a-drop-in-the-ocean-you-are
48. Leadership Circle Profile™ and Universal Model of Leadership™ are created and owned by The Leadership Circle®.

49. Profile Interpretation Manual, The Leadership Circle®, Version TLC 10.1, p.11.
50. Leadership Circle Profile™ is created and owned by The Leadership Circle®.
51. Profile Interpretation Manual, The Leadership Circle®, Version TLC 10.1, pp.59,69,75.
52. Taylor Jenkins Reid, https://www.goodreads.com/quotes/8671342-people-think-that-intimacy-is-about-sex-but-intimacy-is
53. Profile Interpretation Manual, The Leadership Circle®, Version TLC 10.1, p.69.
54. Godin, Seth, 2008, *Tribes*, Penguin Publishing Group, Kindle Edition, location 688.
55. Dr. C Otto Scharmer, "Leading from the Emerging Future. Minds for Change – Future of Global Development Ceremony to Mark the 50th Anniversary of the BMZ Federal Ministry for Economic Cooperation and Development November 13, 2011, Berlin", https://www.ottoscharmer.com/sites/default/files/2011_BMZ_Forum_Scharmer.pdf
56. Global activists, https://www.contiki.com/six-two/young-activists/
57. Befeqadu Hailu, https://www.thebookseller.com/news/befeqadu-hailu-named-international-writer-courage-2019-pen-pinter-prize-1096671
58. Memory Banda, https://www.euronews.com/2019/12/11/we-must-not-let-fear-stop-us-young-women-share-stories-of-activism
59. Robert K. Greenleaf, 2002, *Servant Leadership, A Journey into the Nature of Legitimate Power & Greatness*, Paulist Press, p.27.
60. Ibid
61. Rick Tamlyn, 2013, *Play Your Bigger Game: 9 Minutes To Learn, A Lifetime To Live*, Hay House, Inc., p.37.
62. Leadership Circle Profile™ is created and owned by The Leadership Circle®.
63. Profile Interpretation Manual, The Leadership Circle®, Version TLC 10.1, p.41.
64. Profile Interpretation Manual, The Leadership Circle®, Version TLC 10.1, p.43.

65. Leadership Circle Profile™ is created and owned by The Leadership Circle®.
66. Chris Argyris, http://www.telusplanet.net/public/pdcoutts/leadership/argyris.htm
67. Martin Luther King, Jr., https://mlk.wsu.edu/about-dr-king/famous-quotes/
68. Philip Shepherd, 2017, *Radical Wholeness: The Embodied Present and the Ordinary Grace of Being*, North Atlantic Books, p.10.
69. Sitting in the fire is a term coined by Arnold Mindell and the title to his book *Sitting in the Fire: Large Group Transformation Using Conflict and Diversity* in which he talks about the art of conflict resolution.
70. Ronald Heifetz, 1994, *Leadership without Easy Answers*, Harvard University Press, p.184.
71. René Descartes, https://www.britannica.com/quotes/biography/Rene-Descartes
72. Betty Sue Flowers, C. Otto Scharmer, Joseph Jaworski, Peter M. Senge, 2005, *Presence: Exploring Profound Change in People, Organizations and Society*, Nicholas Brealey Publishing.
73. Betty Sue Flowers, C. Otto Scharmer, Joseph Jaworski, Peter M. Senge, 2005, *Presence: Exploring Profound Change in People, Organizations and Society*, Nicholas Brealey Publishing, Kindle Edition, Chapter 14, "Science Performed with the Mind of Wisdom", location 2492.
74. Robert Kegan, Lisa Laskow Lahey, 2016, *An Everyone Culture, becoming a Deliberately Developmental Organization*, Harvard Business School Publishing, p.27.
75. Jaworski, Joseph, 2012, *Source: The Inner Path of Knowledge Creation*, Berrett-Koehler Publishers, Kindle Edition, location 64.
76. Ibid, location 163.
77. Howard Washington Thurman, https://www.goodreads.com/quotes/6273-don-t-ask-what-the-world-needs-ask-what-makes-you
78. Viktor Emil Frankl, 1993, *Man's Search for Meaning*, Buccaneer Books.
79. Richard Barrett, 2016, *A New Psychology of Human Well-Being: An Exploration of the Influence of Ego-Soul Dynamics on Mental and Physical Health*, Lulu.com, p.123.
80. Profile Interpretation Manual, The Leadership Circle®, Version TLC 10.1, p.49

81. Leadership Circle Profile™ is created and owned by The Leadership Circle®.
82. Profile Interpretation Manual, The Leadership Circle®, Version TLC 10.1, p.53.
83. Sharon Daloz Parks, 2005, *Leadership Can Be Taught: A Bold Approach for a Complex World*, Harvard Business Review Press, Kindle Edition, location 479.
84. Robert J. Anderson, William A. Adams, 2019, *Scaling Leadership: Building Organizational Capability and Capacity to Create Outcomes that Matter Most*, Wiley, p.1, p.10.
85. Ryan Holiday, When the System Breaks Down, Leaders Stand Up, https://dailystoic.com/marcus-aurelius-leadership-during-a-pandemic/
86. Ronald Abadian Heifetz, Martin Linsky, 2002, *Leadership on the Line: Staying Alive Through the Dangers of Leading*, Harvard Business Press, p.225.
87. Game changer definition, https://www.lexico.com/definition/game_changer
88. David Whyte, 2003, *Everything Is Waiting for You*, Many Rivers Press.
89. Robert J. Anderson and William A. Adams, 2016, *Mastering Leadership: An Integrated Framework for Breakthrough Performance and Extraordinary Business Results*, Wiley, "Two primary movements", p.160.
90. Bob Anderson, https://2y3l3p10hb5c1lkzte2wv2ks-wpengine.netdna-ssl.com/wp-content/uploads/2018/03/No-Safe-Path-to-Leadership-Mar18.pdf, p.4.
91. Richard Barrett, 2015, *The Metrics of Human Consciousness*, Lulu.com, p.43.

Recommended reading

Anderson, Robert J. and Adams, William A., *Mastering Leadership: An Integrated Framework for Breakthrough Performance and Extraordinary Business Results*

Anderson, Robert J., Adams, William A., et al., *Scaling Leadership: Building Organizational Capability and Capacity to Create Outcomes that Matter Most*

Arbinger Institute, *Leadership and Self-Deception: Getting Out of the Box*

Arbinger Institute, *The Anatomy of Peace: Resolving the Heart of Conflict*

Barrett, Richard, *The Metrics of Human Consciousness*

Blake, Amanda, *Your Body is Your Brain: Leverage Your Somatic Intelligence to Find Purpose, Build Resilience, Deepen Relationships and Lead More Powerfully*

Block, Peter, *The Answer to How is Yes: Acting on What Matters*

Daloz Parks, Sharon, *Leadership Can be Taught: A Bold Approach for a Complex World*

Flowers, Betty Sue, Scharmer, C. Otto, Jaworski, Joseph and Senge, Peter M., *Presence: Exploring Profound Change in People, Organizations and Society*

Ford, Debbie, *The Dark Side of the Light Chasers: Reclaiming your power, creativity, brilliance, and dreams*

Frankl, Viktor, *Man's Search for Meaning*

Garvey Berger, Jennifer, *Unlocking Leadership Mindtraps: How to Thrive in Complexity*

Greenleaf, Robert K., *Servant Leadership: A Journey into the Nature of Legitimate Power & Greatness*

Heifetz, Ronald A., Grashow, Alexander and Linsky, Marty, *The Practice of Adaptive Leadership: Tools and Tactics for Changing Your Organization and the World*

Jaworski, Joseph, *Source: The Inner Path of Knowledge Creation*

Jaworski, Joseph, *Synchronicity: The Inner Path of Leadership*

Kabat-Zinn, Jon, *Wherever You Go, There You Are: Mindfulness meditation for everyday life*

Kegan, Robert and Laskow Lahey, Lisa, *An Everyone Culture: Becoming a Deliberately Developmental Organization*

Kegan, Robert and Laskow Lahey, Lisa, *Immunity to Change: How to Overcome It and Unlock the Potential in Yourself and Your Organization (Leadership for the Common Good)*

Kimsey-House, Henry and Kimsey-House, Karen, *Co-Active Coaching: Changing Business, Transforming Lives*

Kimsey-House, Karen and Kimsey-House, Henry, *Co-Active Leadership: Five Ways to Lead*

Mindell, Arnold, *Sitting in the Fire: Large Group Transformation Using Conflict and Diversity*

Mindell, Arnold, *The Leader as Martial Artist*

Rosenberg, Marshall B., *Nonviolent Communication – A Language of Life: Life-Changing Tools for Healthy Relationships*

Shepherd, Philip and Brown, Jeff, *Radical Wholeness: The Embodied Present and the Ordinary Grace of Being*

Tamlyn, Rick, *Play Your Bigger Game: 9 Minutes to Learn, A Lifetime to Live*

Zohar, Danah and Marshall, Ian, *Spiritual Intelligence: The Ultimate Intelligence*

Acknowledgements

THANKING ALL THE people who made an impact on me so that I could make this book a reality would be a very long list. So long that it would probably exceed the length of the book itself.

Instead, I'll have to make a conscious choice and name the coaches, mentors, friends and family members who kept coming to my mind, heart and soul in the very key moments of creating this book that (once again) re-created me.

To Karen Williams, my book mentor who kept compassionately challenging me. Thank you for sharing your wisdom, your heart and your loving feedback. You helped me edit and re-edit some of the hurting parts of my life, bringing me so elegantly in touch with my own boldness.

To Phil Askew, Ronnie Clifford, Antony Parry, Rick Tamlyn, Dori Ben-Chanoch and Angelique van Dam, my Co-Active coaches and leadership mentors who, all in their different times and roles, walked beside me throughout my journey. In fact, I wish to thank to entire Co-Active Training Institute for the magic that you bring throughout your coaching model. While I've learnt other models, concepts and philosophies in the course of my development, your work awakened in me what made everything else possible - aliveness.

To Liberto Pereda, VP Europe of The Leadership Circle®, for the heart, soul and wisdom put into this work and community. The unimaginable depths of the Universal Model of Leadership unfold so easily in every conversation with you.

And then to my dear friends. Jela Begonja Kovacevic, for showing me the power of selfless support and heart in a relationship with others. Our conversations make us both bolder. Emilie Cymberg, for showing me the power of intelligent mind and deep intuition. You made me feel a true citizen of the world with a second home in London. Nuria Pomes Raventos and Meritxell Blasco, for showing me that leadership is not a lonely business.

To all the friends and respected colleagues who shared their praise for this book and supported its final form through their honest feedback.

To my family for the three key whys that made this book possible. My husband, for teaching me why to take risks. My mother for teaching me why to have discipline. My father for teaching me why to have passions.

To my stepson Jan, for teaching me the art of accepting others.

And finally, to my son Noa. Thank you for teaching me the depth and the breadth of love and trust. Before you, I thought those levels were unreachable for me. Seeing you, I know I merely write about bold souls. You *are* one.

About the author

ZANA BELIEVES IN the transformative power of bigger, bolder conversations. Bold leaders, having the sixth sense of speech, are accountable to initiate those conversations, thus taking a personal risk in the service of making their world better.

That is why bolder conversations are also the essence of her work with executives and C-suite leaders in the area of coaching and leadership development. Zana is the founder of Bold Leadership Culture, an EU-based company that offers leadership development solutions to clients worldwide taking their individual and collective leadership to the next, bolder level.

She is a Certified Professional Co-Active™ coach, Co-Active leadership graduate, Organisation and Relationship Systems Certified coach and Leadership Circle® certified practitioner. She holds a bachelor's degree in languages, a master's degree in Economics from the University of Zagreb (Croatia), and an MA in International Business Administration from Leeds Beckett University, UK.

Zana lives in Zagreb, Croatia and works internationally as a leadership coach, consultant and speaker. She is a mother and a stepmother, a wife and a daughter who believes that to live is to learn. And to live is to rebel from a place of love in the service of change.

Learn more at:
www.boldleadership-culture.com
www.linkedin.com/in/zanagoicpetricevic